From Chaos to Ambiguity

"Caring for culture requires all of us to pay attention. In some cases we are called as deep cultural missionaries to seek grace and authentic expressions in the marginal arenas, dark 'suspect' realms of culture. Jeremy has been such a faithful ambassador of Christ to punk and noise music. Now we get to read about his years of experience listening, pondering, and beholding, with a discerning theological lens, the nuance and depth of these cultural products and artists who created them. This book is a guidepost for those who dare to dive into the depth of murky cultural waters, and create something entirely New into the world. Jeremy has given us a rare and much needed gift for all who endeavor and choose to love the margins of culture, to mend the soil of culture for the next generation."

—**Makoto Fujimura**, artist, and author of *Art+Faith: A Theology of Making*

"Jeremy Hunt is here to drive a rusty spike through the flimsy bubble housing the concept of God as perfection. With careful examination and the honesty of lived experience, he finds pain, dirt, and disgust in the imperfect blasts of sonic savagery from his favorite noise rock bands, who exemplify weird joy and cockeyed hope, catharsis in getting one's hands dirty, getting to work, and making a racket—all with an ear toward enlightenment."

—**Ryan Masteller**, writer and editor, founder of Critical Masses, bylines at Tiny Mix Tapes, *Tabs Out Cassette Podcast*, and *Cassette Gods*

"*From Chaos to Ambiguity* is poetic, constructive, and, frequently, brilliant. Indeed, there exists nowhere in my knowledge such a comprehensive collection of interviews and first-hand accounts of noise rock, which opens all kinds of generative theological possibilities. This work stands out as a singular, substantive contribution to the theological discourse on popular music. I highly recommend it."

—**Kutter Callaway**, William K. Brehm Chair of Worship, Theology, and the Arts, Fuller Theological Seminary

"Avid explorer, devotee, and practitioner of noise rock, Jeremy Hunt brings to the forefront the concerns and practices of its prominent artists. Highlighting the poignancy of their thundering woes, *From Chaos to Ambiguity* declares dehumanizing forces present in our time. Thus, as a theological quest, the book honors noise rock's emancipatory powers where God is tangibly accessed through community, performance rituals, palpable waves of feedback, and distortion. Here, the human howl becomes a gateway to the soul. As a work of musicology, the book catalogs the lyrics, philosophies, and developmental histories of noteworthy noise rock bands. In doing so, Hunt models commitment, Christian involvement with God's world and its creatures."

—**Maria Fee**, artist, professor of theology and culture, The Seattle School of Theology and Psychology

From **Chaos** to **Ambiguity**
A Theology of Noise Rock

WRITTEN BY
Jeremy Hunt

☙PICKWICK *Publications* • Eugene, Oregon

FROM CHAOS TO AMBIGUITY
A Theology of Noise Rock

Copyright © 2024 Jeremy Hunt. All rights reserved. Except for brief quotations in critical publications or reviews, no part of this book may be reproduced in any manner without prior written permission from the publisher. Write: Permissions, Wipf and Stock Publishers, 199 W. 8th Ave., Suite 3, Eugene, OR 97401.

Pickwick Publications
An Imprint of Wipf and Stock Publishers
199 W. 8th Ave., Suite 3
Eugene, OR 97401

www.wipfandstock.com

PAPERBACK ISBN: 979-8-3852-0401-4
HARDCOVER ISBN: 979-8-3852-0402-1
EBOOK ISBN: 979-8-3852-0403-8

Cataloguing-in-Publication data:

Names: Hunt, Jeremy [author].

Title: From chaos to ambiguity : a theology of noise rock / by Jeremy Hunt.

Description: Eugene, OR: Pickwick Publications, 2024 | Includes bibliographical references.

Identifiers: ISBN 979-8-3852-0401-4 (paperback) | ISBN 979-8-3852-0402-1 (hardcover) | ISBN 979-8-3852-0403-8 (ebook)

Subjects: LCSH: Rock music—History and criticism. | Popular music—Religious aspects. | Spirituality in music. | Music—20th century—Philosophy and aestehtics. | Music—21st century—Philosophy and aestehtics.

Classification: ML3921 H868 2024 (paperback) | ML3921 (ebook)

VERSION NUMBER 10/25/24

All quoted lyrics and album art included are used with permission from their respective bands and/or artists. No rights claimed on those elements.

Scripture quotations are from New Revised Standard Version Bible, copyright © 1989 National Council of the Churches of Christ in the United States of America. Used by permission. All rights reserved worldwide.

To April:

Then, now, and always . . . great hearts beat alike

Contents

Preface | ix
Acknowledgements | xv
Introduction | xvii

1 The Beauty of the Ugly | 1
2 Punk to Noise: A Brief History | 19
3 What Is Noise Rock? | 34
4 Confusing Talk of Love with Love Itself: *Oxbow* | 51
5 Let's Go to Heaven in a Big Rowboat: *God Bullies* | 75
6 All Roads Lead to Embodiment | 95
7 A Theology of Noise/Rock | 115

Epilogue | 141

Appendix: Music Timelines | 145
Bibliography | 149
Discography | 153

Preface

PLAYLIST:

"30,000,000,000,000,000 People"—Part Chimp

"Heal the Weak"—Big Business

"Swavay"—Shakuhachi Surprise

"Clown Pain"—Brandy

"Monkey Chow Mein"—Cherubs

"This Is Love"—Buñuel

"All This And Everything"—Celan

Scan for Playlist

PREFACE

To fully grasp the weight and impact music has had on me, I have to take you on an abbreviated journey of my development as a listener of music and as a musician. I've been captivated by music for nearly as far back as my memories can reach. My first impressions were two-fold: the *Star Wars* double-vinyl soundtrack album and *Rhapsody in Blue*. Starting at the age of four, I sat for hours with the liner notes of the *Star Wars* score playing on my parents' record player, memorizing the photos as the music washed over me and reading about this far off planet of Tatooine and trying to picture what was actually happening in a movie that I wasn't old enough to see. I was obsessed with John Williams's work.

At this same time, I was being slowly introduced to classical music, in part thanks to my parents homeschooling me and trying to instill in me some sort of appreciation for the "classics" and in part thanks to Bugs Bunny cartoons (if you know, you know). I'm sure some of it took root in a subconscious way that I'll never be able to fully identify or pinpoint. But *Rhapsody in Blue* got my attention in an unexpected way. It was, in the vernacular of a kid, fun. Here was a big, boisterous, lively, nuanced, delicate, moving piece of jazz (What was jazz, I wondered at the time? Even the name made it sound like a blast.) that was a joy to listen to from start to finish. And remember that a nearly 20-minute piece of music is a lot for a kid in single digits to stay focused on. But it grabbed my attention and never completely let go.

Fast-forward a few years and my diet was mostly rock staples on the oldies radio station in Easley, SC. Like most kids in that framework, my mind was blown when I realized that you could combine orchestral music with rock, thanks to "Strawberry Fields Forever." I had been taking piano lessons for a few years at that point, learning Bach, Beethoven, Chopin and others, so having a somewhat intimate knowledge of the workings of classical music helped make that impact even stronger, knowing just a hint of the juggling needed to bring those worlds together. Towards the end of my piano lessons, I gained enough hubris to say that I was tired of only playing what had come before and asked my teacher for some lessons about composing. It takes a lot of stupidity to think that you're fed up with learning Rachmaninoff, but there you go. I composed my first piano piece for the recital that year and then it was off to France...

At this point, I was over halfway done with high school when my family was moved to Clermont-Ferrand, due to my dad getting a new assignment at Michelin. Musically I was starting to explore more modern

PREFACE

rock sounds, but they were largely filtered through the Christian music scene, so instead of listening to grunge or alternative rock, it was dc Talk's *Jesus Freak* and Newsboys' *Take Me to Your Leader* and Audio Adrenaline's *Some Kind of Zombie*. Thanks to the relocation to Europe however, my doors were about to be blown off, so to speak, as I was exposed in quick succession to four massive albums released in 1997: Daft Punk—*Homework*, Oasis—*Be Here Now*, The Verve—*Urban Hymns*, and U2—*Pop*. Coupled with French rap and immigrant music from bands like Zebda, my musical world was wide open and my brain and ears felt like a melting pot of sounds and impressions. I got my first glimpse of noisy punk music through hearing a friend's band play at bar during Clermont's annual Fête de Musique and at that point, everything was on the table. I had shifted from a framework where only certain types of music were "safe" for consumption by good Christian people to one where it was virtually impossible to not hear other perspectives and styles. It was so liberating . . . once again, I was captivated. Rather than segregating myself from the rest of humanity through unnecessary dichotomies, this art was reuniting me with myself and others.

This growth and transformation continued as I returned to the States. When I was a freshman at Davidson College, just north of Charlotte, NC, I started working with Young Life, a para-church organization. My heart was bent towards helping high school students, particularly those who didn't really fit in to any easy social grouping. This inevitably led me to punks and metalheads, teens who spent their free nights and weekends at venues in Charlotte, dives like the Milestone and Tremont Music Hall. It was through Young Life that I met a scrawny kid named Ron. He and I struck up a friendship and though he never ended up coming to a single YL meeting or camping trip, I still look back fondly at the times we shared together. For me, it was always about building the relationships, regardless of the "outcome."

Ron was the kid who said that if he ended up coming to a YL meeting that he'd probably rip a page out of the Bible to use to roll a joint. I laughed at that, even though he was likely being serious. I told him that he'd always be welcome, and in return, he introduced me to the music scene that he loved: punk, hardcore, and heavy rock. We went to a few shows together and these gigs became parts of my first introduction to the world of heavy music. At these shows I found people of all walks of life, unified by a passion and zeal for bands and art that were confrontational but also communal.

PREFACE

Growing up in a conservative part (also known as "most of the state") of rural South Carolina, I was raised in the Reformed Presbyterian tradition. The churches I attended as a kid, while filled with loving people, were quite inflexible when it came to questioning elements of the faith. Or perhaps it would be more accurate to say that they were inflexible towards questions about doctrine and systematic theology. Everything in its right place, if you will. As I grew older, I continued to have several pressing questions that never found a welcoming ear: Why can't women preach? Why are the gifts of the spirit absent from the modern body? Is homosexuality a sin? The list goes on. The answers I received from those church leaders tended to be rather short and I found them lacking. There were also several situations of great suffering visited upon other members of the church that felt mostly ignored: a twelve year-old boy committing suicide, a teenage girl with mental disabilities being sexually abused, a marriage counselor who was married and the father of seven children having multiple affairs with his patients. While I know now that there often isn't an easy answer to suffering, the nonresponse from leaders within the church felt deafening.

In the process of wrestling and seeking answers, I found hope, rest, and peace in the world of heavy music. These genres tend to be open to questions, without judgment or threat of being labelled a heretic. This isn't to paint them as absolutely perfect communities, but they offered me something that, at the time, I couldn't find in church: acceptance for who I was in the moment and a solidarity to stand shoulder to shoulder with me as I continued my journey. This was a second conversion, if you will. A place where I got saved from empty religion, found Jesus anew, and found my people, my family. In this way, I suppose you could say I fall in line with the argument that Ben Quash is advancing in *Found Theology: History, Imagination, and the Holy Spirit*. I was able to find God in a series of new parameters, even as I was still walking in faith amongst a church family.[1] My love of this intersection of music and faith even brought me to a message board community where I met the woman who would later become my wife and several friends who I'm still in contact with nearly two decades later.

There are few moments as potent as throwing yourself at another human being, colliding in violence, joy, passion, and frenetic energy. In the pit, all become equal. In the thundering bass lines, the pummeling drumming and interweaving guitar riffs, there are moments where I have seen beyond myself, where my place in humanity and the universe becomes crystal clear.

---

1. Quash, *Found Theology*, 6.

PREFACE

I am humbled, emboldened, overcome, and transfixed, as music rises, crests, and crashes, wave after wave hitting me in an almost tangible fashion. I have lived through a few key moments of transcendence in my life . . . and several of them have taken place at metal and hardcore shows: Codeseven, Aria, Torche, Further Seems Forever, The Beautiful Mistake . . . the list goes on and on and once again, captivation.

These themes continue up through the present with the formation of new communities. One such loose collective, centered around Twitter, arose through the efforts of Seth Werkheiser, a creative/writer/artist who's become a friend through the process. In 2011, Seth started a nerdy metal trivia Twitter account called Skulltoaster. Each week, Monday-Friday, he posted a single trivia question centering around a metal band, musician, label, album or song. He did that for about six or seven years and in that time, he became a sort of godfather of "#nicemetal" on Twitter. People from all over the country and beyond now participated in what amounts to on-line trivia games. As goofy as the concept might sound (and it definitely is), through my participation, I've connected with so many people, other individuals who've found hope and inspiration through heavy music. Here's the striking thing: many of them have similar stories of struggling with faith and discovering a home within the communities that rise up around the bands/scenes in these genres. That community has since morphed and mutated into other collectives, including #MetalBandcampGiftClub, an email and Discord-based group that focuses on generative acts of kindness, wherein strangers and friends alike buy albums for each other, thus supporting bands themselves and spreading the love of weird, heavy, and experimental music across the country and around the globe.

In many ways, this is the story of how I nearly lost my faith when traditions and restrictive practices choked all the life out of it, and how I found new life through throwing myself into music and noise . . . and finding the presence of God in the feedback and distortion.

Acknowledgements

There is no way in which these acknowledgements could adequately thank the people who helped bring me to this point. The stories and communities that converged to support, encourage, challenge, and motivate are far too numerous and I am too deeply in their collective debt. With that in mind, I simply offer up my humblest and most sincere thanks to the following people . . .

From the Fuller community: Kutter Callaway has not just been a mentor and advisor, but he has become a friend that I admire and respect. I am so grateful for his wisdom and insights, from the first class I took with him until now. For Rob Johnston and Cathy Barsotti, I am eternally thankful that our paths first crossed years ago at Young Life staff training. Their compassionate approach to life, theology, and culture was exactly what I needed to experience then and I am lucky to have continued experiencing it in the years since reconnecting with them at Fuller. To Maria Fee and Mako Fujimura, thank you. Each of you opened up doors of understanding and opportunities to be heard, giving a self-doubting musician the kick in the ass needed to actually create something with confidence, overcoming years of struggle and hurdles in the process.

To my friends and fellow sojourners at Fuller: Julia Hendrickson, Dea Jenkins, Brianna Kinsman, Chris and Carly Lopez, September and Ivan Penn, Eric and Julie Tai, Tamisha Tyler, Steven Vrendenburgh, Jasmine White, and Diana Wilburn, thank you for being incredible conversation partners, asking tough questions and providing so many opportunities to wrestle with what we all hold dear. I am humbled by your respective gifts and talents and consider myself lucky to be in your orbits.

ACKNOWLEDGEMENTS

To my brothers in QOHELETH: Mike Strickler and Caiden Withey, you are two of the most talented men I've had the privilege of knowing. Gratitude doesn't even begin to cover what I feel when I think of each of you and the art we've been lucky enough to create together. The fact that I get to count you as two of my dearest friends underneath all of that is something that I marvel at regularly. Thank you for going on our consistently weird adventures with me. I hope that what we've forged together makes you proud.

To Toxic Waste Buzzkill: y'all are an incredible group of creatives, musicians, and artists. It's been a blast building this community with you and I can't wait to see what the future has in store for all of us.

To my parents: thank you for constantly pushing me into the streams of art and music. I don't know if all those piano lessons and museum visits paid off in the ways that you initially envisioned, but you lit a fire that burns brightly to this day and is now being passed down to your grandchildren and spreading to their friends around them.

Lastly, none of this would have even gotten off the ground without the love, support, patience, encouragement, and partnership of my wife, April. If I struggled forming the thoughts above, words absolutely fail me here. You know me inside and out, better than anyone else on the planet. You are my constant and you saw these things and starting calling them out of me years before I got there myself. This ridiculous adventure has only been possible because of you. I will never be able to fully express what you mean to me, but I'll spend the rest of my life desperately trying, failing, and trying again: I. Love. You.

To my daughters, Flannery, Eloise, Blythe, Maeve, and Delia: Dad's finally done. Thank you for all the patient nights and weekends you sacrificed so I could write one more paper or read and underline one more book. I pray that this journey opens doors for all of us to go on more adventures together. I love you into the noise and back, on all the wavelengths that we can hear and beyond.

Introduction

This text asserts that noise rock is a culturally significant and vital subgenre of rock music, that it offers multiple starting points for theological dialogue and engagement, and provides a launch pad for a noise-facing theology that opens us up to be more fully human and engaged with the world. Because we're going to be covering a multitude of sounds and bands that criss-cross several decades in American music, a roadmap of where we're headed will likely be helpful. In chapter 1, we explore the nature and feel of noise rock by providing various gateways for listening to the music itself, from both leading noise rock bands and more obscure artists within the genre. Why is noise rock compelling and why does it matter? Chapter 2 includes a very brief genealogy of the genre by way of its "ancestors," punk and no wave, in order to identify what common threads are found in all three genres and what aspects are unique to the formation and sound of noise rock. This chapter in particular leans heavily on outside voices and perspectives on those ancestral genres, as there are a few oral histories that have been collected over the years from the people who were actually there as the music formed and reverberated on the East and West coasts of the US. I purposefully chose to give them a wide berth within the chapter to help properly frame everything that comes after in the rest of this work.

From there, in chapter 3 we venture into a historical overview of noise rock, highlighting the pioneers of the genre and how they carved new paths musically within the United States. In tandem with that exploration, we also wrestle with the ontology of noise itself and the ways in which it functions when combined with music and musical structure (or lack thereof).

INTRODUCTION

At this point, we take all that has come before and apply it in-depth to two key bands within noise rock, Oxbow and God Bullies, in chapters 4 and 5. Each group receives their own focus within their respective chapters, looking into their histories, the conceptual themes that each wrestled with throughout parts of their discography, and closing with various frameworks for interpreting that work theologically.

Finally, we close out this noisy journey, first with a look at how noise rock intersects with three vibrant strains of theology: transgression, liberation, and weakness in chapter 6; and second with a conclusion that attempts to build out an actual theology of noise/rock in chapter 7. This constructive theology is focused on four key elements: active ears, empathetic hearts, attuned minds, and new tongues. Each of these is meant to bring together noise/rock and theology in ways that are mutually beneficial, celebrating what noise rock offers up to our existence, while encouraging a broadening and deepening of what a generous and humane theology could look like in conversation with the genre.

If we seek out the *Sonus Dei* wherever it might be heard, I believe that one of its centers might just be noise rock . . . if we have ears to hear, hearts that are quick to be patient, minds that are willing to understand, all while forming fresh language for engaging with the people and communities around us.

Chapter 1
The Beauty of the Ugly

PLAYLIST:

"Hitting the Wall"—Cows

"Visible Cow"—Barkmarket

"Who Was in My Room Last Night"—Butthole Surfers

"Mouth Breather"—The Jesus Lizard

"Release the Bats"—The Birthday Party

"Scrape"—Unsane

"The Talking Horse"—Melvins

Scan for Playlist

I woke up today, this morning
I'm bloody, I'm beaten
I find that I have been robbed
They took my shoes, my wallet
I'm still drunk, I say "fuck it"
I go to my job

Then my boss, he fires me for no
   good reason
No reason at all
He says, "if you come back I will call a
   policeman"
I'm hitting the wall

So I call home, say "dad, I'm robbed
I'm fired, I need money, I need
   money bad!"
He says, "That's bullshit! You're lying!
   I know you!
Need money? Too fuckin' bad!"

He says "son, you gotta get out there and
   fight, man!
Compete and stand tall"
I say "dad, that's the trouble with your
   whole damn white man
I'm hitting the wall"

So I'm walking, there's kids behind me
They're laughing, they throw rocks at me
I start running, they chase me
They're coming, they're gaining
They're gonna get me

Now there's no answer to this I can
   think up
I'm taking a fall
I duck into a bar, sit back and drink up
I'm hitting the wall

Then later three big guys
They poke me, they wake me
They say, "boy you'd better pay"
I pull out my pockets
They don't laugh, they punch me
They kick me, I'm out the hard way

I'm laying by a dumpster drunk
   and beaten
With nothing at all
People point at me and say I'm sickening
I'm hitting the wall

"Hitting the Wall"—Cows[1]

---

1. Cows, "Hitting the Wall."

THE BEAUTY OF THE UGLY

It smells like hell inside here
too thick to clear your ears,
or your head
Are you being led?
Just try not to cry
not to hide
Sonny listen how I survived
I survived

I bought a handgun made out of glass
I cut a hole in the side of a wild ass
I made a window of copper and string
then I took aim its intestines, I say

Something moving out there
Can't you see it shaking
In the, in the, in the wind

It tastes like fear around here
too close and too revered
to make out what I'm heading for

Dance
Mule

Something moving out there
can't you see it shaking
in the, in the, in the wind

Dance
Mule
Dance
Dance
Dance

"Visible Cow"—Barkmarket[2]

What hits you first is the distortion-laden guitar. Thick, heavy, a wall, a tangible presence. Coupled with an end-of-the-world bass line, this feels like an auditory bull in the china shop, a wrecking crew hellbent on bulldozing your eardrums, stirrups, hammers, and anvils. Galloping drums threaten to overwhelm the entire affair, filling the sound spectrum AND THEN... Shannon Selberg's howling shrieks pierce through the mix and you realize that we're only just getting started.

"Hitting The Wall" follows the woes of an outcast, a member of society who's barely tolerated by the people he encounters. Indeed, he's only tolerated inasmuch as he's able to perform the duties expected of him or capable of paying what he owes to debtors, to society's critics, the ones in power by virtue of being born in that position (or having enough money to buy

---

2. Barkmarket, "Visible Cow."

it). Our narrator isn't one of those folks. He's less than, worn out and trod upon, bloody and beaten.

And that's how his day starts. It only goes downhill from there.

Cows, *Peacetika* (1991)

* * *

The sound of a couple of car doors being shut.

A click, possibly of a stereo being turned on.

The single strum of a jangly, slightly out-of-tune guitar. The fragile notes allowed to barely ring out and flutter in the air. The cracked voice of David Sardy starts meandering, almost muttering about hell and its smell, air too thick to hear or breathe or something. It's overwhelming . . . and then the guitars. Again with the guitars. But this time Sardy's vocals are front and center. The guitars are off in the distance, stretched out over some desert landscape, as are the trash can drums that swoop in to join them as Sardy continues to recite some sort of fever dream about a glass gun, a hole cut in the side of an ass, and other surrealist images.

It's not until the 1:05 minute-mark (a third of entire song itself) that the music comes in full-force, mixed in a way that the average listener is used to hearing. But at that point the brilliant impact has been made. Everything clicks at once and you're brought fully into the madness of Barkmarket and everything that it entails. You're told that this is the taste of fear and maybe that makes sense and maybe it doesn't, but you're along for the ride until it calms down or it crashes and burns and honestly, either result feels like it would be completely satisfying.

Barkmarket, *Visible Cow Single* (1996)

FROM CHAOS TO AMBIGUITY

* * *

Why start a discussion of noise rock here? With these two bands and these two songs? There are other bands in the genre with far greater fame and/or notoriety, and, perhaps hand-in-hand with those qualities, greater impact on the genre as a whole. Bands like Swans and Butthole Surfers and The Jesus Lizard and The Birthday Party and Unsane and even Melvins (when they expanded their grunge/metal sound into something weirder and more experimental). These bands are deeply formative and foundational to the sound and ethos of noise rock, yet they were not among my first, personal experiences with the noise. That honor goes to "Hitting The Wall" and "Visible Cow."

This would probably be a good juncture to mention that, for all the meaning that this art form has brought into my life, I have often found myself with a similar mindset towards noise rock as Daniel A. Siedell has for modern art:

> But I stand before you incapable of justifying my relationship with modern art, theologically or otherwise. All I can do is confess that I cannot imagine my life as a human or as a Christian without it: that it has made a claim on me, and that God has graciously worked through that claim.[3]

I am at the same mercy of noise rock. It has a claim on me and I am so thankful for everything and everyone it has brought into my life over the years. It is as simple (and as massive) as that.

Thus, at the risk of sounding grandiose, I believe that, by entering into this music and these genres, we have the opportunity to join in God's work as outlined by Jeremy Begbie in *Voicing Creation's Praise*: "In creating a reality distinct from himself and allowing it a measure of genuine freedom, God risks exposing himself to the pain and rejection it can bring. The divine love takes the risk of getting no return for its expense."[4]

I don't think it's an easy process to expose ourselves to potential pain and rejection, but yet again, I think this is a way in which the heavy genres of music can actually embody a movement of faith. Or to once again call on Begbie: "To view the cosmos as proceeding in one smooth, continuous crescendo towards eternal perfection is palpably naive; the

---

3. Siedell, *Who's Afraid of Modern Arts?*, 8.
4. Begbie, *Voicing Creation's Praise*, 170.

physicist today reminds us that the world, in temporal terms at least, is heading for a fairly bleak future."[5] As I mentioned above, there needs to be room for this loss, this lament. Things do look (and indeed often are) bleak. But there is an important turn:

> There needs to be an interaction with creation, a development, a bringing forth of new forms of order out of what we are given at the hand of the Creator. And there will be a redeeming of disorder, mirroring God's redeeming work in Christ, a renewal of that which has been spoiled, a re-ordering of what is distorted. This redeeming activity will entail a penetration of the disorder of the world—human and non-human, just as the Son of God penetrated our twisted and warped existence.[6]

This is the power of heavy music, in my humble estimation: speaking truth to power, carving out room for lament, asking difficult questions and finally, providing the space for all of those things in creation to interact with the Creator. It's a long way from playing heavy riffs and head-banging to abstract noise rock fueled by the punk ethos, but I think it's a journey worth taking.

So what of the songs at the beginning of this chapter? As I was exposed to heavier and more eclectic music, I stumbled across Barkmarket thanks to Riley Breckenridge of Thrice and Cows thanks to Jesse Matthewson of KEN mode (who I had initially checked out due to a recommendation from Breckenridge, so thank you, Riley for unlocking the trajectory of my listening and playing habits for the past ten to fifteen years). In much the same way that *Star Wars*, *The Wiz*, *Rhapsody in Blue*, "Strawberry Fields Forever," *Homework*, *Be Here Now*, Creedence Clearwater Revival, The Mars Volta, and so many other musical milestones made their mark on me, these two blasts of noise rock snapped so many things into place for me when I heard them for the first time. Taking cues from punk, metal, rock, and even hardcore, noise rock is the misfit stepchild of all four styles. A misfit that might find its literary voice in the writings of folks like Flannery O'Connor and Philip K. Dick. As O'Connor is rumored to have said, "You shall know the truth and the truth shall make you odd." Noise rock is odd music for odd people. As a musician in a noise rock band, it fits my sensibilities like a broken in pair of Chucks.

And it's where I've found my artistic home.

5. Begbie, *Voicing Creation's Praise*, 174.
6. Begbie, *Voicing Creation's Praise*, 179.

Ultimately, one's motivation for putting music in conversation with theology comes down to what one believes is happening in cultural expressions (or traces) and what one believes about the movement and the work of the Spirit (pneumatology). Let's start with my convictions for the former, and then we'll tackle the latter, concluding by bringing the two together.

According to Kathryn Tanner, humans are made by their culture, but they also make their culture. It's a give-and-take, symbiotic relationship that we will see throughout the music/theology discussion. Tanner suggests that culture is a defining mark of human existence, a pattern of behaviors and practices that help us define boundaries, tell stories, examine our own lives, and much, much more: "Culture is understood as a human universal. All (and only) human beings have culture. Culture is the defining mark of human life."[7] Additionally, it is through our varied and voluminous cultural expressions that the full scope of what it means to be human is put on display. "Though culture is universal in the sense that all people have one, the anthropological use of the term highlights human diversity."[8]

Culture, broadly speaking, is a central location for meaning-making, wherein we often try to put experience under the microscope of the artistic creative process and wrestle with what we believe about the world outside and ourselves inside. It is the water in which we swim and it is the water itself that we are trying to study and reckon with. Bill Dyrness suggests that, "The aesthetic desires and the habits and objects that embody these are fundamental to our human identity."[9] Furthermore, he writes, "Culture is always what we humans make of creation. That is, there is always something of the goodness of creation in human creation, however distorted this may be."

There are massive, "capital C" Cultures and then a myriad of smaller cultures and subcultures and probably even sub-subcultures. Being aware of them and their influence on us (and our own influence back onto them) is vitally important. It makes us better citizens of this planet and better setters of the communion table. If we know what connects with our neighbors (and with ourselves), we can craft better invitations, more knowledgeable starting points for discovery that open up discussions with our communities.

---

7. Tanner, *Theories of Culture*, 25.
8. Tanner, *Theories of Culture*, 26.
9. Dyrness, *Poetic Theology*, 8.

As a result, studying our own cultures within the US is a needed and crucial endeavor. It is so easy to write off that which we do not understand in our culture as "the media" or "Hollywood," or any other number of sweeping generalizations. Taking the time to grapple with why a particular movie or song or TV show or piece of fine art resonates across political or socio-economic lines (or perhaps, why it strikes a chord with a certain demographic and not others) is a way of demonstrating love to our brothers and sisters around the country. Understanding culture, much like learning how to more helpfully read and interact with Scripture, is a means of "reading" humanity. Is it possible to grapple with major issues of our era without being able to engage with film and music and books? Absolutely. But does that skill add nuance and depth to one's comprehension of those same issues? Undoubtedly. I can't begin to count the number of conversations that have opened up over the course of my life due to a mutual interest in a TV show or a book or a musical artist. Those shared experiences allow for a sort of shorthand communication between mutually engaged parties and they're often an in-road for building friendships and relationships. How many BuzzFeed quizzes must already exist to help you figure out which character from *The Office* you are? For better or worse, we often identify with such-and-such a character from this comedy on Hulu or that drama on Netflix. If we know that someone also connects in a similar way, it can be an automatic point of connection for present and future dialogue.

Much of the work in theology and culture over the past few decades has focused on film and TV, and with good reason. Both mediums are enormously popular. Streaming platforms are everywhere and consumption of visual storytelling has completely captivated us in the US. *LOST, The Sopranos, Breaking Bad, Stranger Things, Game of Thrones*, the Harry Potter series (books and films), the Marvel Cinematic Universe, and more are all examples of movies and TV shows that have completely dominated the national conversation, sometimes for years at a time. I would argue that part of being a good steward of what we've been given from God is spending the time to understand the creative impulses and thematic threads that draw us into stories that so deeply captivate our imagination.

But what of music? How do we grapple with this art form? This is what I hope to examine here, specifically by focusing on one genre, noise rock. Broadly speaking, I think that music offers a certain space for reflection and introspection that inherently visual forms like film and TV do not. Much of the spiritual/theological examination of music up to this point has focused heavily on lyrics (and with good reason, as that gives an immediate footing for wrestling with intent). If I might wax poetic for just a moment, I think that music can function like a time machine, allowing us to step into a Ricoeurian understanding of the flow of time, and prolong the present moment for longer than a breath. Music also allows us to move forwards and backwards, envisioning possibilities for the future, and revisiting key moments from our past with stark clarity and realism.

With that in mind, I hope to explore the space within music where we can sense the movement of the Spirit, the presence of God, and eventually, understand how lament and humor can be embodied in the specific genre of noise rock. Begbie has a well-known example of how music can illuminate deeper spiritual truths about God, using a triad chord to demonstrate how a triune God can exist, three-in-one. The chord is made up of three individual notes, yet becomes something else entirely when all are played together. They are themselves and something more all at the same time. If you understand this basic concept of music, it can immediately shed light on a difficult theological concept that might be hard to grasp in other frameworks.

As for the work of the Spirit, this is where I lean heavily on the insights of mentors like Rob Johnston, Bill Dyrness, and Kutter Callaway. As we go through this exploration, I will periodically refer to elements of music, whether it's a performance, an entire album, a song or perhaps some related ephemera (album art, liner notes, packaging, and so on) as a "trace."[10] This is a crucial term that I have adopted from several years of studying under Callaway, and which he in turn credits to Maeve Louise Heaney in her examination of Arvo Pärt's *Spiegel im Spiegel*.[11] It's a concept that he explores in his book, *Watching TV Religiously*, and in that volume it's used primarily in the context of TV shows and their episodes (and the sometimes fleeting manner in which they are available for viewing):

> We prefer the term "trace" instead of "text" to describe this common thread because it more accurately reflects the complex, dynamic, and ever-accruing form of meaning-making that takes place in our interaction with audiovisual media (which also include film, web videos, etc.).[12]

---

10. Callaway and Batali, *Watching TV Religiously*, 16–17.
11. Callaway and Batali, *Watching TV Religiously*, 204.
12. Callaway and Batali, *Watching TV Religiously*, 16.

While the term "text" is certainly appropriate for the lyrics and liner notes side of music, similar to its inadequacy in the face of the multifaceted nature of TV, it barely covers the richness and depth of what music has to offer, as well as the ephemeral nature of the experience of listening to a song or album. A quote often attributed to Jean-Michel Basquiat captures the very nature of that fleetingness, by saying that "Art is how we decorate space, music is how we decorate time."[13] This makes "trace" the perfect term for the various music pieces that we'll be encountering in the chapters ahead.

Poetic theology, as expressed by Dyrness, makes room in our understanding of the presence of God in the artistic, in the cultural spaces. His approach is a generous and giving one, an understanding of the movement of the Spirit in and through the culture-making habits of people. He sees these habits as expressions of love that help point to deeper longings, even if those making these cultural traces don't necessarily ascribe to a specific faith tradition. He makes the case that these traces and our love of them helps carve out space and light for us to eventually see and interact with the Creator:

> Poetic theology intends to reverse this order of things: it insists that we start with the cultural artifacts, especially those symbolic practices and experiences around which contemporary persons orient their lives. Scripture and tradition are thus constantly reread in the light of the human drive to create a beautiful life. It is crucial that this be understood as an active and imaginative process.[14]

As for Johnston's contributions to this field, his work in film and theology is essential to any well-rounded discussion. His books on movies and faith are foundational to theology and culture conversations, while his recent work, *God's Wider Presence*, will prove to be indispensable for my work in music. In short, Johnston makes the case that the work of the Spirit has never been limited by the "people of God," but rather that it moves when and where it wants. Wisdom and insights into the heart of God, he suggests, come from the Spirit and show up inside and outside of the community of God's people. This would suggest that wisdom can take many forms, including the chaotic and satirical clothing of noise rock:

> We need a hermeneutic that includes not only Scripture and the tradition of the church but also cultural receptivity and human

---

13. Ciocca, "Basquiat Decorates Time and Space."
14. Dyrness, *Poetic Theology*, 294.

experience. Scripture and the theological formulations of the church past and present cannot be ignored, but neither can the witness of our culture and our own personal experiences.[15]

The farther I get into my studies of theology and culture, the more I'm convinced that the healthiest option for putting these two fields in conversation with one another is to start from the bottom-up. As Johnston puts it,

> We seek out certain kinds of knowledge, but in other areas we remain tentative and/or uninterested. In particular, we fail to take seriously the importance theologically of the cultural signs of the times—"the shared environment, practices, and resources of everyday life." We fail to discover God in the midst of life.[16]

Start with a descriptive analysis of the trace and its unique context of creation and realization and you will likely end up situated for a much more beneficial dialogue than if you worked prescriptively from the top-down. In his book *Poetic Theology*, Dyrness has one of the most beautiful explanations that I've encountered for this approach. He recommends that we allow the individual symbolic practices and experiences of every person's life to inform and illuminate Scripture and tradition (Church and communal). He suggests that this gives life to our spiritual imaginations and breathes fresh life into both the sacred texts and our long-held practices. "And this, after all, is the final secret of poetic theology: To have eyes to see through this country to the place where there is space and light enough, where we will live in God."[17]

Additionally, by calling on insights from Philip Stoltzfus, Dyrness argues that theology is like music: it allows for propositional expressions, but comes alive the most when given space to take root through embodied performance:

> Stoltzfus thinks that theology is like music: while embodying various traditional formulations, it "resists satisfactory expression in propositional form." This is because, as in drama or music, theology is more naturally embodied in various performances.[18]

So to that end, bottom-up engagement with cultural traces allows us to take each trace on its own terms, rather than risk dismissing or overlooking

---

15. Johnston, *God's Wider Presence*, 15.
16. Johnston, *God's Wider Presence*, 38.
17. Dyrness, *Poetic Theology*, 312.
18. Dyrness, *Poetic Theology*, 293.

something via a top-down approach. For this reason, my methodology begins with that bottom-up, descriptive approach which provides for a more enriching experience overall. It allows us to encounter an album, song, or band in their element, expressing themselves as they are first and foremost, listening fully to what they have to say and gleaning as much of their creative and communal context as much as possible. Then, and only then, once this work has been done, we can begin to assess, interpret, and wrestle with what's being offered up to us by way of that music. It also helps prevent a certain amount of hypocrisy that the American Church is sadly known for. This might be a clichéd example at this point in time, but I remember vividly when certain groups of Christians (particularly those who view cultural topics as a battlefield that must be won) went out of their way to make excuses for why viewing the R-rated *The Passion of the Christ* was permissible, yet all other R-rated films should be considered off-limits for true God-fearing believers. Rather than making sweeping judgment calls about an entire segment of films made for mature viewers, it would be a much more judicious exercise to weigh each of the films on their own terms.

I can already hear the objections to this approach, namely that it would take too much time and that it's easier to just segment one group of trace expressions off to the side and not have to worry about them, for the sake of spiritual integrity or what have you. And yes, that's true, to a certain extent. The top-down approach is a lot less time-consuming and a lot easier mentally and spiritually. You're able to push aside whatever doesn't fit within that a preset framework and focus on what does. Johnston argues that we're stuck in a centuries-old dichotomy that needs breaking:

> Still encumbered by the inheritance of seventeenth-century thinking—of the dichotomous subjective/objective trap—we have found ourselves unable to hear the testimonies and entertain the call for new thinking with regard to God's revelatory Presence. Somehow, piety needs again to be connected to theology—to be given personal content. A third way—one that recognizes God's revelatory Presence in and through life in its fullness—is called for.[19]

I agree completely with Johnston that a third way is needed. In fact, I would push further and argue that this isn't being a good steward of the resources we've been given by God . . . and it's also not a Biblical model (in the sense that it doesn't model what we see in Scripture).

---

19. Johnston, *God's Wider Presence*, 41.

Let's look at each of those two assumptions, that generous cultural engagement is too time-consuming and that we can only hold onto some semblance of spiritual integrity if we practice a form of cultural avoidance. If we imagine that we're like the servants who've been tasked with taking the talents that God has given and using them to help grow and nurture his kingdom, what does it say about us if we decide that certain stories and traces can simply be lumped together in an ad hoc way and thus pseudo-evaluated en masse? How would we be any different from the one who buried the talents given out of fear of messing up? Whether it's the easy target of movies with a certain rating or music with profanity in the lyrics, won't the boss be upset at us if we risk engaging and sowing those talents, instead of safely burying them and focusing on something else?

And yet, I would assert that that's exactly what we're invited to do: venture into the riskier traces, moving in the Spirit to encounter the Spirit there in the unseen and the mystery. What if we spend our entire lives on the sidelines of these experiences and don't realize what we've missed? This is what Johnston says can happen when we don't take cultural traces seriously: we miss finding God in the midst of life. This is tragic. What if we're so scared of offending God that we avoid a multitude of opportunities to encounter God in the weird and broken artistic expressions that surround us every day through our screens, books, and earphones? To lean once more upon Johnston's wisdom and experience:

> It is not Christology, but pneumatology, that provides the primary direction and insight for our theological explorations. If we are truly trinitarian in our theology with regard to God's revelation beyond the walls of the church, are we open also to moving from Spirit to Word in our theological pilgrimage, as well as from Word to Spirit? And more particularly, are we open to the testimony of the Spirit of Life in and through creation, conscience, and culture, as well as the work of the Spirit of Christ in redemption? It is the same Spirit.[20]

This is what leads me to the second of my two assertions: choosing not to engage descriptively drifts away from the examples we see in the texts of the Bible. These are stories and people that are messy and violent and tragic and funny and miraculous and despairing and hopeful and disastrous and prophetic and deeply, deeply human. I fear that we sometimes read Scripture (and traces) looking so hard for God and the exact thing that we think

---

20. Johnston, *God's Wider Presence*, 17.

God wants us to do in any given situation that we completely miss how free the people within these stories are to be broken and relentlessly human. This is what good art can do (and indeed, part of what I think makes art good): open us up to encountering God where we least expect, among the people where we least expect it. This is one of the major through-lines of the Biblical texts and it's something that our brothers and sisters on the frontlines of liberation and public theology have been telling us for decades.

God is found in the margins and in the messiness of life. Approaching the cultural expressions of our day and age descriptively frees us to see each one with fresh eyes . . . and by extension, the possibility of encountering God with fresh sight. Fortunately, there are musicians who grasp this on an almost intuitive level (at least if they're being honest in their art and craft), which is why you can have a band like Thrice, with their lead singer and lyricist Dustin Kensrue, who has consistently wrestled with his faith throughout the band's existence, yet doesn't ostracize the rest of the band for not sharing the exact same beliefs (indeed, their internal relationships are based on something deeper: friendship and brotherhood). They simply create their music organically and let what they have to say flow naturally out of that.

Art of Noise or the Noise of Art?

One of the biggest hurdles of our upcoming journey into Noise Rock will be, by necessity, the looming presence of noise itself. While we will tackle a brief history and evolution of the genre shortly, at the risk of being painfully obvious at the outset, there's a very good reason why "noise" is included in the name. It is a messy field of music, where certain rules and standards are tossed out the window. Some of them return, and some of them we will never hear from again. Perhaps paradoxically, the invitation presented by noise is to become a more attentive and patient listener, which I believe has profound implications for us as we navigate the particular moments that we are collectively experiencing in the twenty-first century. Through our screens, our technology, our various news outlets, a myriad of streaming platforms (both video and audio), we are beyond inundated with information and certain forms of sensory feedback.

Part of what we're constantly being presented with, through all this input, is how we want to engage with that very input, as sometimes the question of whether we actually want to isn't even an option, especially in public spaces. I suppose cloistering ourselves away might be a plausible solution, though it doesn't seem like a tenable one for very long if you actually hope to live in a healthy community with others (or plan to get married and/or have kids). But what if we could learn to gain a better appreciation of noise? And/or develop a more discerning ear that helps us sort through what we're hearing?

This will be the final piece of the puzzle that we examine at the end of the exploration ahead: the ontology of noise and how it helps us build a theology of noise rock. Since it will be a bit before we get there and we have many paths to walk in that direction, here are a couple of key thoughts from Paul Hegarty, a professor, experimental musician, and author, to give us the start to a foundation:

> For now, I want to argue that noise happens to "me," is beyond my control, and somehow exceeds my level of comfort with the soundworld I or we inhabit. In some way, noise threatens me, is part of the other I define myself against. Noise is a phenomenology of noise, insofar as it exists in relation to individuals, who define themselves as being subject to noise (a community forms around the hearing of a house or car alarm).[21]

This idea that noise is something beyond our control is deeply important, on both a temporal, human level and on the Divine plane. If we are incapable of controlling noise or stopping its existence in its entirety, then our options for engagement will have to get much more creative than simply trying to silence it or shut it out. Furthermore, noise itself is contingent on other circumstances beyond its own control. In some ways, the manner in which Hegarty talks about noise next is reminiscent of apophatic theology, discussing primarily what it is not:

> Noise . . . does not exist independently, as it exists only in relation to what it is not. In turn, it helps structure and define its opposite (the world of meaning, law, regulation, goodness, beauty, and so on). Noise is something like a process, and whether it creates a result (positive in the form of avant-garde transformation, negative in the form of social restrictions) or remains process is one of the major issues in how music and noise relate.[22]

---

21. Hegarty, *Noise/Music*, 4.
22. Hegarty, *Noise/Music*, 5.

If the sound of the Divine is music, are we the noise? To borrow from Frederick Buechner, if there's no room for noise in the relationship with God, there's no room for me.[23] Conversely, perhaps it's not an either/or, but a both/and. God as both noise and music? And every expression from humanity within that spectrum is an attempt to both reconnect with God and/or wrestle with the disconnect of the finite from the infinite?

To be clear, I am not suggesting that we continually summon as much noise as possible as constantly as possible and then never give our ears, brains, and souls a chance to rest. Peace and quiet are both desperately needed and should be sought out on a regular basis. But what I am proposing, at least in part, is that a better understanding of noise, how it functions, and how we might better engage with it, will lead us to clearer heads in the midst of the storms. Once we are attuned to the frequencies of noise, we are no longer strangers with it and it can lead us home, when the vibrations and rhythms match our own.

Returning to Hegarty's definitions of noise, I want to quickly draw upon three key patterns of noise I encountered as a kid. I grew up in the foothills of the Appalachian Mountains, in the area of South Carolina commonly referred to as the Upstate. My childhood and teen years were marked by the recurring presence of three noises that visited themselves upon me, whether I wanted them or not: summer storms, cicadas buzzing, and dirt track race cars. The storms are pretty self-explanatory; the sound of pouring rain on our roof, the flash of lightning followed quickly by the crack-boom of thunder . . . but then it was often followed by the cool stillness of the air after a system had moved over our neighborhood. The cicada often roared so loudly that I could fall asleep to the waves of sound coming in through the screen of my window when I opened the glass. I've often joked that it was the rural, country version of hearing the ocean waves flow in and out with the tides. Lastly, the well-worn track of the Greenville-Pickens Speedway. I've never been into racing and I never attended a race at this speedway. Yet it was only three miles from my house and whenever it was racing season, the low rumble of the cars would carry, ebbing back and forth depending on where the drivers were on the track.

None of these sounds were ones that I would have chosen to help define my childhood and yet they have stuck with me on a primal level

---

23. Buechner, *Alphabet of Grace*, 47: The full original quote: "Without somehow destroying me in the process, how could God reveal himself in a way that would leave no room for doubt? If there were no room for doubt, there would be no room for me."

throughout my life. To this day, the sound of cicadas brings a stupid grin to my face immediately. It's the sound of home, the sound of life bursting out of the ground and reminding us collectively that this planet doesn't belong solely to us. The noise goes where it wants and how it wants.

This then is the framework within which I will be working throughout this exploration. Music and noise have intrinsic value from the ground up. Transgressive art, including noise rock, has intrinsic value from the ground up. This isn't a question of dichotomies, with some things being measured unclean and off limits and some things being clean and safe for listening consumption. Life is messier than that, and if we're willing to be honest with ourselves and God, faith is messier than that. Understanding and grappling with that messiness doesn't require separation, but rather a willingness to engage and wrestle with it. This is what Noise Rock offers: an artistic, creative, and embodied juncture for the mess.

Chapter 2
Punk to Noise
A Brief History

PLAYLIST:

"Ramblin' Rose"—MC5

"Judy Is a Punk"—Ramones

"I Wanna Be Your Dog"—Iggy Pop

"We Got The Beat"—The Go-Go's

"Six Pack"—Black Flag

"The Glory of Man"—Minutemen

"Orphans"—Teenage Jesus and the Jerks

"Tunnel"—Mars

Scan for Playlist

In order to fully grasp where noise rock operates and how it first arose, we need to properly understand the two genres that helped give birth to it: Punk and No Wave. For the sake of time and space, this chapter, which focuses on these two streams, won't be exhaustive. The history of each is simply too rich and deep at this point to attempt such a fool's errand. That said, some overview is necessary simply for perspective and to try to give credit where it is due. For that reason, here are some parameters: when speaking about "Punk" in this chapter, I will be referring to the initial waves of that genre that found expression in the New York City and Los Angeles areas in the late 1970s and early 1980s. There were other centers of punk elsewhere around the world, but these two locales were influential enough that the ripples of their impact are still being discussed and written about. Furthermore, when discussing "No Wave," I will largely be talking about the initial response in NYC to the first wave of punk in that scene. There are examples of "No Wave" elsewhere, but again, this was an epicenter of that activity and provides the table setting we need to serve up the main dish of noise rock after this chapter.

To help give this part of my exploration a framework, I lean heavily on the reporting and storytelling of three key texts: *Please Kill Me: The Uncensored Oral History of Punk* by Legs McNeil and Gillian McCain, *We Got the Neutron Bomb: The Untold Story of LA Punk* by Marc Spitz with Brendan Mullin, and *No Wave* by Marc Masters. The first two books use the oral history approach and format to tell the stories of their respective punk scenes (NYC and LA), while Masters's volume mixes interviews and oral history with commentary and reflection from the author himself. In essence, both punk books are essentially living, breathing timelines made up of the direct quotes of the people who were actually there. Oral histories with little preamble or framing devices can be a bit bracing, as there's not much to help ease the reader into the deeper waters. They can feel like being dropped into the deep end of the pool from about two stories up, yet they are invaluable to capturing the feel of what was happening during these heady, messy times. Further, by bringing *No Wave* into conversation with those two books, it offers insight specifically into the musical repercussions of punk and where some musicians took it in its immediate aftermath.

I'm hoping to help split the difference here, providing some broader context and key takeaways amongst the key quotes and stories. The first takeaway: while Punk eventually evolved into a genre known for more political stances and social commentary, the initial forays into the sound of

Punk were primarily built on traditional rock motifs: sex, drugs, hard and fast living.[1] The music side of it was equally moored in tradition: faster chord progressions, more distortion, discordant vocals, but largely structured in a similar fashion: verse, chorus, verse, chorus, bridge, etc.[2] In other words, it was something you sing (or shout) along to, if you wanted. Highlighting these aspects is not in anyway meant to take away from the legacy or impact of these scenes or musicians. But rather this is a distinction that's necessary to mark in order to help show the development of Punk as it matured, changed, warped, and mutated. No Wave emerged as both resistance to the continued excesses of rock as expressed by Punk and a call to further deconstruct and dismantle the approach to the music and/or noise. What follows in the rest of this chapter is a work of curation. It is meant to represent a guided tour of some of the key archival interviews of this era, in order to better situate these primary sources in a larger historical narrative. As a result, emphasis has been placed on allowing each of these voices to be heard in larger, more complete segments. From there, I draw connections between the parts and the whole. Subsequent chapters will shift back toward a more interpretative mode of engagement, but only after this descriptive work has had space to provide a more insightful starting point.

Punk

So with all that said, what exactly was going on in NYC, LA, and elsewhere as Punk was forming? No less than Andy Warhol himself knew that "something revolutionary was happening. We just felt it. Things couldn't look this strange and new without some barrier being broken."[3] Ron Asheton, guitarist for the legendary Stooges (a.k.a. Iggy Pop and the Stooges) experienced this tidal wave of change firsthand:

   1. "Punk started in the 1960s with garage bands like the Seeds and Question Mark and the Mysterians. Punk is just real good basic rock and roll, with really good riffs—it's not like boogie rock. It's not very embellished, intricate music—it's not with the synthesizers, it's just real basic 1950s and early 1960s rock" (Nancy Spungen in McNeil and McCain, *Please Kill Me*, 282).
   2. "I mean, basically punk rock was just rock and roll. We weren't taking music anywhere new. What a lot of people would have to understand is we were all at the age where we had grown up with pop radio: Buddy Holly, the Everly Brothers, Little Richard, and Chuck Berry. So it wasn't that the music was new, it was a return to the three-minute song" (Eliot Kidd in McNeil and McCain, *Please Kill Me*, 281–82).
   3. McNeil and McCain, *Please Kill Me*, 16.

> The audience weren't cheering; it was more like animal noise, howling. The whole room turned really primitive—like a pack of starving animals that hadn't eaten in a week and somebody throws out a piece of meet. I was afraid. For me it wasn't fun, but it was mesmerizing. It was like, "The plane's burning, the ship's sinking, so let's crush each other." Never had I seen people driven so nuts; that music could drive people to such dangerous extremes. That's when I realized, This is definitely what I wanna do.[4]

Wayne Kramer, lead guitarist for MC5 (another proto-punk band from Michigan, like the Stooges), recalls a sense that something wasn't right with the world, with this music playing a role in pushing back. He reflected, "We knew the world generally sucked and we didn't want to be a part of it. We wanted to do something else, which amounts to not wanting to get up in the morning and have a real job."[5] MC5's iconic debut album, *Kick Out the Jams*, begins with an intro that sounds downright religious in its fervor, calling upon brother and sisters to start a revolution, asking if they're ready to testify.[6]

In the midst of punk taking shape, there was a sense of something vital happening. And the people who it attracted were a weird and wild bunch. Rejects and kids who didn't fit in at home. Dope smokers, anarchists, political radicals, and illiterates. Poet, activist, and musician Ed Sanders reflects how some of it sprang out of a history of family trauma and rejection:

> So there developed another kind, more of a lumpen hippie, who really came from an abused childhood—from parents that hated them, from parents that threw them out. Maybe they came from a religious family that would call them sluts or say, "You had an abortion, get out of here" or "I found birth control pills in your purse, get out of here, go away." And those kids fermented into a kind of hostile street person. Punk types.[7]

For Danny Fields, manager of The Stooges and the Ramones, the political connections and inspirations of punk were also pretty clear from the outset. He surmised that the establishment of the White Panther Party, an antiracist collective of which MC5 was a part, was influenced by

---

4. McNeil and McCain, *Please Kill Me*, 34.
5. McNeil and McCain, *Please Kill Me*, 47.
6. MC5, "Ramblin' Rose."
7. McNeil and McCain, *Please Kill Me*, 22.

black radical musicians and politicians. Bobby Seale and Huey Newton and Eldridge Cleaver were their political heroes. Albert Ayler, Sun Ra, and Pharoah Sanders were their musical heroes. It was a Midwesternized version of anarchy. Tear down the walls, get the government out of our lives, smoke lots of dope, have lots of sex, and make lots of noise.[8]

Punk made rock even more human, more broken, and more accessible. It didn't make things perfect, as sexism, misogyny, and homophobia were still very present.

But it upended portions of the music and cultural scene by being less interested in toeing the established party line of the music industry. And it gave its participants a sense of place and belonging. As Cheetah Chrome expressed, relaying a sentiment from his Dead Boys bandmate, Stiv Bator, "Stiv kept saying, 'Listen, in New York they're into what we're into. We're not weirdos there. We'd be normal there.'"[9] For David Johansen of the New York Dolls, that sense of accessibility was part of his band's legacy. "People who saw the Dolls said, 'Hell, anybody can do this.' I think what the Dolls did as far as being an influence on punk was that we showed anybody could do it. . . . We were bringing it back to the street."[10] That attitude quickly translated to other bands, providing the punk scene with a sense of lineage in a very short time, one that even transcended national boundaries. Fields recalled how the do-it-yourself spirit jumped from the Dolls to the Ramones and then to The Clash.

> But Paul and Mick weren't in The Clash yet, but they were starting it. They were afraid to play until they saw the Ramones. I mean, Paul and Mick told the Ramones, "Now that we've seen you, we're gonna be a band." The Ramones said, "You just gotta play, guys. You know, come out of your basement and play. That's what we did." Basically the Ramones said to them, which they said to countless other bands, "You don't have to get better, just get out there, you're as good as you are. Don't wait till you're better, how are you ever gonna know? Just go out there and do it." That's what the Ramones got from the New York Dolls, you know, "What are we waiting for?" To me that's the important part of it, what bands pass along to other bands by way of confidence.[11]

8. McNeil and McCain, *Please Kill Me*, 49.
9. McNeil and McCain, *Please Kill Me*, 255.
10. McNeil and McCain, *Please Kill Me*, 128–29.
11. McNeil and McCain, *Please Kill Me*, 253–54.

While many of those initial punk bands still relied on label support for recording and marketing purposes, the budgets they were working with were much smaller in comparison to the established rock bands of the day. As Joey Ramone recounted,

> We did the album in a week and we only spent sixty-four hundred dollars making it. . . . Some albums were costing a half-million dollars to make and taking two or three years to record, like Fleetwood Mac and stuff. Doing an album in a week and bringing it in for sixty-four hundred dollars was unheard of.[12]

Given all the other systems it was questioning, it probably shouldn't be surprising that Punk also wrestled with frameworks of meaning and belief. Was it enough to simply upend what had come before? Several musicians reflected on how punk/art rock singer/songwriter Patti Smith in particular embodied these questions and practices. Her drummer, Jay Dee Daugherty, described it as a process where Smith

> came to grips with her own spirituality and some sort of spiritual system. I think she didn't feel that way anymore. This something I've not talked to her about, this is my own observation. She was working out some theme of resurrection and coming to a different place.[13]

Musician and author Jim Carroll concurred:

> I always found Patti to be very Christian—very, very Christian. I mean, we didn't go to church or anything, but she would read stuff from the Bible. People talk about, "Jesus died for somebody's sins but not mine," but to me she was always Christian. I don't know, maybe she knew I was this Catholic kid and I never really lost that. I mean, I love the rituals of Catholicism. I hate the fucking politics, and the pope and shit, but the rituals of it are magic. I mean, the Mass is a magic ritual, for God's sake, it's transubstantiation, and the stations of the cross—I mean a crown of thorns? Getting whipped? It's punk rock.[14]

Smith's longtime personal assistant, Andi Ostrowe, also found Patti's incorporation of faith iconography and themes to be intricately tied up within the art she was making. She recalled,

---

12. McNeil and McCain, *Please Kill Me*, 251.
13. McNeil and McCain, *Please Kill Me*, 327.
14. McNeil and McCain, *Please Kill Me*, 327–28.

> That time reminded me of the movie Still Moving that she made with Robert Mapplethorpe.... She's blindfolded as the film starts, and she starts talking about being in the darkness, and about going into the light. She starts reading from the Bible, and at the end she says, "I choose life." I think her whole premise is that you can't be stopped by the darkness, you have to take the light force and go with that because that's the force of life, that's the force of God, that's the force of art and creation.[15]

With all the upheaval and constant exploration happening during this period, perhaps it shouldn't come as a surprise that this movement was bound to splinter and fragment, implode and simultaneously seep and spread into the cultural cracks around the country and the globe. It was the sound and style of a bunch of artists and musicians trying to tear things apart, but perhaps not having the bearings they needed to make sense of what they were building afterward. Or maybe not having the energy after all that dismantling to actually start rebuilding? Canadian director and screenwriter Mary Harron was part of the NYC punk scene in the early days of her career, working as a music journalist. Her thoughts on it perfectly depict the exhausting push and pull of tearing things down and starting something from the ground up:

> I felt like everything was new. There were no definitions, or boundaries, it was just moving forward into the light, it was just the future—everything new, no rules, no nothings, no definitions. "What are we? We don't know." It wasn't for years that I realized it was nihilism. Or whatever.[16]

Before too long, it appears that punk was already played out, DOA even as it was catching on outside the NYC center. Or at the very least, it felt that way to some of those, like Legs McNeil, who felt a sense of ownership about its formation and development. The chaos they had unleashed was beginning to get tamed, beginning to feel commonplace, and it didn't sit well with him at all...

> After four years of doing Punk magazine, and basically getting laughed at, suddenly everything was "PUNK!" I was in Los Angeles, staying at the Tropicana and hanging out with the Ramones and Alice Cooper, when the Sex Pistols landed in Atlanta. It was very bizarre, because as the Pistols made their way across America,

15. McNeil and McCain, *Please Kill Me*, 377–78.
16. McNeil and McCain, *Please Kill Me*, 315.

and the hysteria was broadcast on the news every night, kids in Los Angeles, and I imagine the rest of the country, were suddenly transforming themselves with safety pins, spiked haircuts, and ugliness. I was like "Hey, wait a minute! This isn't punk—a spiked haircut and a safety pin? What is this shit?"[17]

But what was happening on the West Coast? If Punk in the Big Apple was already close to being chewed up and spit out, how was the City of Angels taking to the genre? If it started mostly in New York, how would it survive elsewhere? Or would it? For writer and music historian Greg Shaw, "Following the theory that if New York punk was about art, and London punk about politics, LA punk was about pop culture, TV, and absurdity."[18] Given the antagonism that was already at the heart of Punk, it shouldn't be a shock to learn that lines were quickly drawn between West Coast and East Coast, divisions based more along socio-economic lines, rather than musical styles (at least initially). Performance artist and musician Bibbe Hansen (and incidentally, Beck's mom) boiled down one of the key differences in an extremely succinct manner: "New York Punk was all about these lower-middle-class white kids suddenly becoming smart-asses. There were always more garage bands here in LA because we have more garages."[19] Some of the reactions also came down to timing, with members of the LA punk scene like Trudie Arguelles-Barrett feeling like NYC had become stale in the same moment that Los Angeles was coming alive:

> I had moved to New York for a while but had decided I didn't want to stay there after all. LA was much more exciting than New York. It seemed like the scene out here was just being born. When I traveled to New York during the summer of '77, Patti Smith and Television and the Ramones had already been the big thing for a while. It's just didn't seem as much of an exciting, new, growing thing, it had already happened. All the bands were already signed and all their record companies and publicists were just gearing up to try and sell a ton of records to us new kids, record business as usual. The people going to CB's were much older people, but we were all really young. We were just teenagers. It was a new thing for us. We felt like everybody else was just kind of jaded.[20]

17. McNeil and McCain, *Please Kill Me*, 360.
18. Spitz and Mullen, *We Got the Neutron Bomb*, 71–72.
19. Spitz and Mullen, *We Got the Neutron Bomb*, 113.
20. Spitz and Mullen, *We Got the Neutron Bomb*, 113.

Was it self-inflicted? Fields seemed to think so, saying,

> Why build an audience for the Ramones of the Pistols or the Clash? Why institutionalize them if they're just going to be destroyed, if it's their nature to destroy others and to destroy themselves? So the whole thing became a great pile of shit that no one wanted to go near.[21]

And McNeil concurred, reflecting,

> Overnight, punk had become as stupid as everything else. This wonderful, vital force that was articulated by the music was really about corrupting every form. . . . It just felt like this phony media thing. Punk wasn't ours anymore. It had become everything we hated.[22]

In truth, the reality was probably somewhere in the middle: Punk was dead, long live Punk. Thankfully, not everyone had that attitude, especially in the greater LA area. One of the more divisive (and ultimately influential) groups in the area was taking shape in 1976. Black Flag remade the punk genre in their own image; faster, more defiant, ultimately mixing in elements of hardcore and even bits of metal to create their own sound. Their logo, four staggered black bars, with "Black" on top and "Flag" on the bottom, is beyond iconic, having been revered, mocked, parodied, back around again to being revered, and now seemingly ubiquitous within the worlds of heavy music and punk. Rather than worry, at least in the moment, with how punk was being shaped and co-opted, co-founder and guitarist Greg Ginn reflected on how he understood the center of the genre for their existence:

> The songs are more what the band is about, rather than the riots and police and tough-guy attitudes of lead singers and this and that. It's lyrics and the feelings of the music. . . . That's the main thing. In terms of the peripherals, the attitude of do-it-yourself, that kind of thing, not being a remote rock star and having layers of management and record labels and all that—instead, booking your own shows, doing your own publicity if necessary. Not everything has to be so home industry, but being willing to do whatever is necessary and not considering one's self remote, dealing with the guy at the distributor and respecting people for the job that they're doing, not thinking they should conform to some narrow aspect.[23]

21. McNeil and McCain, *Please Kill Me*, 366.
22. McNeil and McCain, *Please Kill Me*, 366.
23. Azerrad, *Our Band Could Be Your Life*, 60.

In the aftermath of their formation and others from the same region that embraced heavier and faster approaches to punk (blending in influences from metal and pushing the tempo of the music in general), the LA contingent of American Punk became more and more fragmented. John Doe of X said that, "People went to the kind of shows that they identified with. There became a more defined rockabilly crowd and a more defined hardcore crowd."[24] Unfortunately, as mentioned earlier in this chapter, all this creativity and overthrowing of genres and expectations didn't always improve things for communities who were already on the margins. Keith Morris, who co-founded Black Flag alongside Ginn, talked about how the hardcore expressions of punk weren't too friendly to female audience members: "We had a sprinkling of female fans. When the hardcore thing really took off, it became more of a macho testosterone overdrive thing, the stage diving and the slam pits. Most girls didn't want to have anything to do with it."[25] Further, The Go-Go's guitarist Jane Wiedlin mourned the changes brought by the expansion of the genre:

> The whole LA scene had changed by the time we got back from England in early 1980, it had been taken over by all these real angry, young white boys, Black Flag. We were like, "What's this all about? It's really gross." We were lumped in with all those stupid bands, but we never even knew those guys. What had started as a scene of girls and gays and stuff was nearly all gone.[26]

Four years later, another group of young men from Southern California would adapt and subvert the punk movement for their own purposes, steering directly into the lean financial tendencies of the early Ramones records. But rather than simply recording the music itself as quickly and cheaply as possible, Minutemen would fashion their own ethos, dubbed *jamming econo*:

> Back then, in the greedy, materialistic Reagan era, making the most of meager resources was positively rebellious. For the Minutemen, "jamming econo" meant parsimonious recording budgets, short songs, and being their own crew. Overdubs were limited to occasional lead guitar lines, studio time was booked for the graveyard shift, and they avoided doing multiple takes, recorded on used tape, and played the songs in the order they were to appear on the

---

24. Spitz and Mullen, *We Got the Neutron Bomb*, 172.
25. Spitz and Mullen, *We Got the Neutron Bomb*, 223.
26. Spitz and Mullen, *We Got the Neutron Bomb*, 234.

album so they didn't have to spend money on editing the songs into the right sequence.[27]

Whereas some of the bands at the epicenter of Punk in NYC had financial support from labels or family members, Minutemen were working class[28] and wore that identity proudly:

> Punk rock was a godsend for their ethics. Maybe even a reward. "Sometimes you have to act out your dreams, because circumstance can get you crammed down," says [Mike] Watt. "And instead of getting angry and jealous of what they got, why not get artistic about it and create a little work site, a little fiefdom. As long as it don't oppress anybody or something, I think it's kind of healthy."[29]

According to Michael Azerrad,

> The hardcore scene was the only place the Minutemen could thrive.... The band's outspoken politics and bargain-basement production values meant they couldn't thrive in the progressive rock scene either. "Put yourself in our place and what else could you be but a punk band?" Watt says. "There was nothing else. No other scene was like that. We would have explored it if there was."[30]

The Minutemen felt DIY was intrinsic to the punk ethos. And yet the key punk bands—the Ramones, Television, the Sex Pistols, the Clash, Wire, et al.—had been on major labels and did little themselves besides make the music. So why did the Minutemen equate DIY with punk? "Because that was our version of punk," Watt says simply. For the Minutemen, punk was a fluid concept—it was things like noticing an ad in Creem for a record by Richard Hell and the Voidoids on the tiny New York indie label Ork Records and calling the number listed. "I called him," says Watt. "I

---

27. Azerrad, *Our Band Could Be Your Life*, 74.

28. "Outspokenly working class, they demonstrated that political consciousness was a social necessity, introducing a cerebral element to the nascent Southern California hardcore scene. They were the band that was good for you, like dietary fiber. The only thing was most people wanted a cheeseburger instead. 'I think one of our problems with radio is that we don't write songs, we write rivers,' Watt once said" (Azerrad, *Our Band Could Be Your Life*, 62).

29. Azerrad, *Our Band Could Be Your Life*, 69.

30. Azerrad, *Our Band Could Be Your Life*, 76–77.

said, 'Is this Hell?' And he said, 'Yeah.' I got scared and I hung up. That, to me, was punk."[31]

No Wave

The fragmentation in sounds and motivations that was happening at this point in LA had already begun in NYC. Almost as soon as punk started feeling played out, a new sound/ethos arose, one that would come to be known as No Wave. Punk had run its course, at least on the NYC front.[32] In response, a series of bands started bubbling up in the area, seemingly drawn to simultaneously converging approaches to music: deconstruction and flaunting musical conventions. If Punk took the roots of rock and cranked the tempos to eleven, charged the vocals into snotty, brash territories, and drove a new wave of fashion and aesthetic style that reached far beyond the music itself, these No Wave bands essentially sought to throw everything into the trash for the sake of making something truly foundation-shaking, unsettling, avant-garde, with disregard for what anyone else might think. Robin Crutchfield of DNA felt that "[No Wave was] a reaction against the Punk music of Brits like The Sex Pistols and all that three-chord rock whose attitudes may have been Punk, but whose musical roots came from Chuck Berry riffs of the 1950s."[33] Lydia Lunch's perspective was even more visceral, as evidenced both by her words and the music she created in Teenage Jesus and the Jerks:

> Nihilistic? The whole fucking country was nihilistic. What did we come out of? The lie of the Summer of Love into Charles Manson and the Vietnam War. Where is the positivity? I'm supposed to be fucking positive? Fuck you! You want positive, go elsewhere. Go find a different lie.[34]

Mars' China Burg found purpose in that nihilism: "It was nihilism in the sense of a rejection of the future.... Nihilism can be rejecting something

---

31. Azerrad, *Our Band Could Be Your Life*, 77.

32. "Punk actually turned out to be as much of a failure as it was a success. In the mid 1970s, the Punk movement stormed the gates screaming, 'Anyone can be a musician!'—this was its success. The face that in the aftermath every asshole in the world became a musician was its failure" (Weasel Walter in Masters, *No Wave*, 5).

33. Masters, *No Wave*, 25.

34. Masters, *No Wave*, 30.

worse than the positives of going along with a disaster scenario."[35] Likewise, musician and label owner Weasel Walter embraced the push of punk's initial impulse of rejection to its logical conclusion:

> Here was a music of violent surrealism, relentless in its aggression, hate and fury, but it was something that truly screamed, "Fuck you all! I don't want to be like you!" Punk said, "Fuck them! We don't want to be like them!" . . . The ideals behind the (anti-) movement known as No Wave were found in many other archetypes before and just as many afterwards, but for a few years around the late 1970s, the concentration of those ideals reached a cohesive white-hot focus.[36]

And that about sums it up. The bands of the No Wave movement were varied in the sounds that they got out of that philosophical and aesthetic motivation, but the idea of negation[37] and annihilation runs through most, if not all, of them. If Punk was life-giving and a breath of fresh air in the way that youthful rebellion can light a fire and offer new perspectives on old assumptions, No Wave was the act of snuffing the candles and seeing what remains in the darkness. Interestingly enough, in his seminal work on the genre, music writer and critic (and a musician himself), Marc Masters notes that "Most of the No Wave musicians and filmmakers were originally artists pursuing painting, sculpture, and performance art. But they decided that New York's music scene was much more vital than its art scene—and much more open to their radical ideas."[38] While there were some overlaps between Punk and No Wave in their shared interest of figuring out new ways of creating music, especially by welcoming in (as if gatekeepers were really given any choice in the matter) artists with little-to-no musical background, No Wave went even farther than Punk in total obliteration of music norms and practices, looking

> back to earlier groups who had truly broken musical rules. Exhibit A was The Velvet Underground. By mixing the noisy rock leanings of Lou Reed, the minimalist drones of John Cale (via his work with avant-garde pioneer La Monte Young), and the art world influence

---

35. Masters, *No Wave*, 31.
36. Masters, *No Wave*, 7.
37. "So No Wave was a movement predicated on negation—except those involved didn't consider it a movement, and didn't predicate it on anything" (Masters, *No Wave*, 15).
38. Masters, *No Wave*, 19.

of Andy Warhol's Factory, this seminal band served as a comprehensive model for No Wave.[39]

Perhaps in a continuation of the inspiration that early white punk bands like MC5 drew from organizations like the Black Panthers, No Wave musicians

> drew on other ancestors from the 1960s and 1970s: the radical noise of free jazz musicians like Albert Ayler and Sun Ra, the experimental blues-rock of Captain Beefheart and the Magic Band, the trance-inducing rituals of German groups like Can and Faust, the screeching art of Yoko Ono and The Plastic Ono Band, and the confrontational performances of Iggy Pop and the Stooges.[40]

In doing so, the presence of these bands that found themselves caught up in this tsunami of noise and, at times, a-musicality,[41] was somewhat narrow compared to the Punk contagion spread around the world. No Wave was "not just a mushroom cloud, but a black hole"[42] that engulfed everything around it with intensity but was all too brief.[43] It burned while Punk itself was still finding its footing outside of NYC, as we saw earlier in its development in the LA scene. Bands like Mars[44] and solo artists like Lydia Lunch[45] were quickly moving from punk influences onto something else entirely.[46] Yet when that something else was found, the bands of this era and genre said what they had to say and then quickly broke up or morphed into new projects.[47] Whether it was boredom or the desire to move on to

39. Masters, *No Wave*, 25.

40. Masters, *No Wave*, 27.

41. "Most No Wave groups used guitar noise, via unusual tunings and primitive techniques, to create texture and mood. The instrument was less a melodic tool than a brush with which to pain abstract sonic pictures" (Masters, *No Wave*, 32).

42. Masters, *No Wave*, 200.

43. "Exactly when No Wave ended is a matter of debate. Some feel it died the day *No New York* was released in 1978, while others contend it survived well into the next decade. Although most of the original groups were finished by 1980, their breakups soon spawned new projects, and many bands inspired by the movement emerged as well" (Masters, *No Wave*, 168).

44. Masters, *No Wave*, 47.

45. Masters, *No Wave*, 74.

46. Masters, *No Wave*, 49.

47. "Any attempt to draw conclusions about No Wave is bound to be frustrating, if not futile. The movement dodged definition, rejected slogans, and embraced contradiction—all in the blink of an eye. The scene, the artists, the music, and the films went by in a flash not because their ideas were small, but because they had the rare courage to move on once their points were made" (Masters, *No Wave*, 200).

new aural spaces to keep pushing artistic exploration forward, the idea of No Wave seemed too concise to last very long.

Yet at the same time, the overall aesthetic impact of the genre was quite profound. Bands like Sonic Youth[48] and Swans[49] took their initial inspirations from the immediate aftermath of No Wave's impact. Their respective interpretations of the No Wave aesthetic and mindset resulted in wildly different sounds. Sonic Youth's oeuvre is characterized by sound collages, elements of improvisation (or seeming improvised parts), and noisy elements . . . all while maintaining a basic sense of musicality that undergirds the entire adventure. Swans, on the other hand, use sound and noise in an elemental and almost primitive way, taking vocal lines or stripped down riffs and repeating and building on them in such a manner that the music itself feels like a physical presence, bludgeoning the listener at length (both within a song and over the course of the entirety of an album). While not strictly No Wave, both bands took key elements of it and brought its beating heart with them into their explorations and thus to new ears and new audiences.

As Masters observed at the end of his journey through this maddeningly brief genre, "Denying solutions and defying limits, No Wave left behind fruitful seeds that contemporary artists continue to explore."[50] And therein lies the trajectory of the path that we will be walking for the rest of this exploration. Noise rock is one of the forests that sprouted from those seeds . . . and we'll dive into that strange, dark terrain next.

---

48. Masters, *No Wave*, 184.
49. Masters, *No Wave*, 190.
50. Masters, *No Wave*, 201.

Chapter 3
What Is Noise Rock?

PLAYLIST:

"I Dreamed I Dream"—Sonic Youth

"Stay Here"—Swans

"Kerosene"—Big Black

"Pepper"—Butthole Surfers

"Nub"—The Jesus Lizard

"Dumbjaw"—Barkmarket

"Tourist"—Cows

"Didn't We Deserve a Look at You the Way You Really Are"—Shellac

Scan for Playlist

WHAT IS NOISE ROCK?

Coming out of the primordial ooze of Punk and No Wave, what then are we to make of Noise Rock? Where did it come from, what does it have in common with its predecessors, and what sets it apart? This is, in some ways, uncharted territory, at least in terms of a genre-wide overview. While books upon books have been written and multiple documentaries have been created exploring Punk and its influence and No Wave has been documented in part through three or four key texts, there are not, to my knowledge, any comprehensive volumes chronicling the development and history of Noise Rock from the ground up. It has been covered through works focusing on specific bands: Butthole Surfers and The Jesus Lizard both have the notoriety and influence to warrant their own films and books. But beyond that, most material on the genre is confined to smaller, cursory surveys. So the goal of this chapter is simply to provide a workable foundation that can be built on (or reacted against) in the future. With that in mind, let's dive recklessly into the chaos, as only the creators of Noise Rock would intend.

If Punk tried to take rock and upend it with speed and copious amounts of attitude . . . and No Wave took that template and threw it out entirely in favor of antagonism, deconstruction, and a general posture of being anti- . . . then I would suggest that Noise Rock looked at the wrecked landscape of pop culture and said, "Fuck it, who cares about any of this," and simply went off to make the loudest racket that it could. Sometimes that includes the deconstruction of No Wave, sometimes the speed and attitude of Punk . . . it almost always includes a solid dose of actual noise and auditory chaos. And usually a healthy disdain for whatever else is going on . . . Come along with us, or don't, it really doesn't matter. We'll be over here doing our own thing because the rest of this posturing sucks.

In that vein, it's possible to see Noise Rock as the culmination of the promise of Punk's attempt to push back against societal norms and demands. While the initial wave or two of Punk offered that as something of an aesthetic ideal, many of those bands were still chasing after some form of success and/or fame. It would probably be too much of a sweeping statement to suggest that none of the Noise Rock bands in existence don't care about success, but the general commitment to find new avenues of expression, regardless of marketability or commercial appeal is one key defining characteristic of the genre, likely taking a page from the No Wave playbook in that respect.

And it only makes sense that those would be two of the key takeaways from Noise Rock's parental units. While The Velvet Underground's 1968 album *White Light/White Heat* is often cited as a proto-noise rock record, I think tracing its lineage to the bands that arose immediately in the aftermath of the No Wave movement makes much more sense, both musically and aesthetically. This is not to suggest that *White Light/White Heat* didn't influence noise rock, but I think the seeds of the genre are more clearly seen in the aftermath of No Wave. As Masters detailed in his book, two groups in particular, Sonic Youth and Swans, formed in the creative ether surrounding No Wave. While he argued that they were not strictly part of the No Wave scene, they were absolutely influenced by it. And I would argue that the unique aspects each brought to the creative process helped drive the approach of Noise Rock, even to this day. Sonic Youth's music is full of deconstructed song structures, sound collages, and manipulated recordings, while Swans' directive is centered on turning music/noise/sound into an imposing, relentless physical presence. Swans' influence on the genre can be felt/heard in the battering rams that are bands like Unsane, Big Black, and Power Take-Off. While the music from these groups is a tad more accessible than Swans, in terms of having hooks and riffs that you can head-bang to, their approaches are also unrelenting and punishing, making the "accessibility" merely a matter of faint degrees. The average pop and/or rock fan would probably still find them to be too much noise and not enough catchy fun.

The influences from Sonic Youth's side of the noise rock equation can most notably be heard in the bands that incorporated field recordings and weird sound samples in their songs. *Musique concrète* is its own genre or subgenre of music (or perhaps more properly described, noise recordings) though there's definite overlap between that approach and the creative output of several key noise rock bands. Groups like Cows, Barkmarket, and Butthole Surfers all used these sorts of non-musical clips and excerpts to varying degrees in their albums. Though to be fair, while Cows and Barkmarket started after Sonic Youth was well underway, Butthole Surfers formed around the same time period (late 1970s/early 1980s). Sonic Youth's first release, the self-titled *Sonic Youth* EP was released in March 1982. Butthole Surfers' debut, also a self-titled EP came out a little over a year later in June 1983. They were also in a completely different part of the country (San Antonio, Texas vs. New York City for Sonic Youth), so tracing an exact lineage of influence (if any at all) is tougher. That said, I do think it's safe to suggest that there was something happening in the creative air of this era that helped lead bands to take extraneous noises and sounds and incorporate them into the musical compositions themselves.

> In a cultural exchange with the youth of Bergenfield I play my noise tape for them. It has Butthole Surfers, Sonic Youth, and a band called Big Black from the Midwest. I advance to my favorite song of the week, "Bad Houses." They hate it—"It's droney." College-radio dirge from the indie labels of America. Nicky tries to be nice, says he likes the drum. Politely, the tape is removed and replaced with Hendrix. Then Bon Jovi. Pensive, Bobby taps my arm. He says, "Look, if you just hang out, you'll see everything, you'll understand what's going on."[1]

> Noise has taken the place of punk rock. . . . People who play noise have no real aspirations to being part of the mainstream culture. Punk has been co-opted, and this subterranean noise music and the avant-garde folk scene have replaced it.[2]

From the outset, there was something about Noise Rock that made it especially off-putting. Famed music critic Robert Christgau called the music of Sonic Youth (among several other bands) "pigfuck" in 1986 in one of his pieces for The Village Voice.[3] The term was likely meant as some sort of a slam, a disparaging way to describe what they were doing musically, yet it does help highlight just how much Noise Rock bands just didn't (and still don't) care about whether their art is well-received or not. As Donna Gaines's quick exchange above details, it wasn't even a matter of demographics or age groups. Being a teen during this era didn't guarantee an understanding or a desire to listen to this music. And as Thurston Moore of Sonic Youth was reflecting on, in embracing that mentality, Noise Rock (and noise by association) took up the middle finger mantle of Punk and truly ran with it.

If any group exemplified that aesthetic in the early days of the genre, it had to be Butthole Surfers. They were, in short, maniacs. The stories surrounding their live performances are the stuff of subversive rock legends. Firing shotguns (with blanks) over the heads of their audiences, lighting instruments on fire, simulating sex acts on stage, playing in front of video screens that were playing footage of medical procedures, absurd amounts of drug consumption . . . all of those scandalous details and hundreds more make up the mythology of the Butthole Surfers:

1. Gaines, *Teenage Wasteland*, 66.
2. Thurston Moore in Sisario, "Art of Noise."
3. Christgau, "Township Jive Conquers the World."

There was a party in East Dallas at a big house in 1981, and we, the Butthole Surfers, and some others played in the living room. It was super loud, so most people were elsewhere in the house or outside. It was the first time I saw Gibby [Haynes, lead singer] do the clothespins in the hair bit. They were amazing to see playing in that small room as smoke wafted through the house and photocopies of cockroaches lying around. Beer spilled all over. Somebody was passing out "acid" that was really strychnine. Clothespins littered the floor. Sweat flew. There was blood. Some people loved it and bathed in the moment. Most were scared and ran away. I picked up a roach from the floor on the way out. It was five a.m. and as I looked back while loading gear into my van, I saw a rifle barrel sticking out of a window upstairs. Turns out the guy that lived up there was a drug dealer and had thirty pounds of marijuana. He was paranoid and tweaking, so his night was filled with terrors.
—Bobby Beeman, Stick Me With Ray Guns[4]

Crazed LSD-fueled punk hippies fr Texas w nude crazed dancing girl, 2 drummers who claimed to be bro/sis, guitarist w his eyes on the next dimension, one nutso bassist after the next, all-American lead singer w hair fulla clothes pins, hand on fire, etc. Insanity onstage w fire and cheap special effects, 6 pair clean sox on rider for all shows. Lived in communal house in Austin when we visited, seemed to take drugs constantly, tour constantly, raised hell and havoc wherever they went. Truly unruly unwashed hallucinating freaks! Their shows were the stuff of legend, where truly anything could happen. They were mining the Texas psych rock of Roky Erickson and 13th Floor Elevators, Doug Sahm, etc and took it waaaay out there. There was rock, there were drugz, there was fire, there was nudity, there was incoherence, there was transcendence, there was crazy, there were hallucinations, there were flashing lights, there was danger. Some of the greatest shows I've ever seen.
—Lee Ranaldo, Sonic Youth[5]

While they were scorching their own cultural path, they managed to continually deconstruct rock music and turn it into their own weird, mutated beast. Their second EP, *Cream Corn from the Socket of Davis*, features a song called "Moving to Florida," with lyrics like:

> Well I'm movin' down to Florida
> And you know I'm gonna have to potty train the chairman Mao

4. Tanner, *Butthole Surfers*, 27.
5. Tanner, *Butthole Surfers*, 107.

And I'm gonna make the governor write my doodoo a letter, child
And then I'm gonna grind me a White Castle slider out of India's sacred cow
Well, I'm goin' down to Florida, child
And I'm gonna build me the atomic bomb
I'm gonna hold time hostage down in Florida, child
Ain't nobody, ain't nobody gonna tell me what to do
Stepchild[6]

As Haynes whisper/drawls his way through the song, it's impossible to know whether these were conceived in a drugged-out state, or perhaps just served up stream-of-consciousness style, but the overall effect is both darkly hilarious and unnerving.

Butthole Surfers, *Cream Corn from the Socket of Davis* (1985)

6. Butthole Surfers, "Moving to Florida."

It's that collision of tone that exemplifies much of the Surfers' work over the years that they were active. It's an almost childlike fascination with the weird and subversive, in one breath focusing on the scatalogical nature of what it means to be human ("I Saw an X-Ray of a Girl Passing Gas") and in the next, deconstructing The Guess Who's huge hit, "American Woman," by stretching it out, distorting the drums into oblivion, and delivering the vocals in a mash of some high-pitched, distressed tones and others shouted through a megaphone.

> Texas is weird and the Butthole Surfers were the kings of Texas weird. Hell, they're the godfathers of modern weird, period. They made it okay to not only do weird but to be weird and put that weird on stage. No matter how weird you got, you would never be considered wilder or weirder than them. They were a true, genuine gift, setting so many artists from that era free. To be weird.—Mike Morasky, Steel Pole Bath Tub[7]

And yet, in spite of all that, or perhaps because of it, Butthole Surfers were met with a fair amount of success in their most active years (after forming in 1981, they've still never officially broken up). Their first full-length record on a major label came with *Independent Worm Saloon*, released in 1993 on Capitol Records.

---

7. Tanner, *Butthole Surfers*, 209.

Butthole Surfers, *Independent Worm Saloon* (1993)

As if having that sort of buy-in from a label wasn't big enough, they also worked with John Paul Jones of Led Zeppelin to produce the album. Accusations of selling out might have worked against lesser bands (i.e., more accessible ones), but no such labelling would work here for these folks. The first track on the album "Who Was in My Room Last Night?" starts out with a bizarre grouping of voices gently chanting, "I'm flying, I'm flying, I'm flying away!"[8] only to be followed up with the pairing of a galloping bass line and a buzzsaw riff on guitar, anchoring the song as Haynes tells us the story of being visited in the middle of the night by some sort of unknown stranger:

---

8. Butthole Surfers, "Who Was in My Room Last Night?"

> The cops, the priest, the crisis line
> No one really had a clue
> No one could tell us who was touching me
> Or exactly what I should do
> My throat was dry, my hopes were high
> But nothing really ever got said
> But who was in my room last night?
> Who the hell was in my bed? Ow[9]

It's an unsettling tale of home invasion and personal space being violated, one that's only enhanced by the visuals of the music video, wherein a rockabilly protagonist is given a drugged drink at a dive bar named "Den-O-Sin" and proceeds to have multiple nightmarish visions (real and animated). The Surfers commitment to their own warped artistic vision showed no signs of weakening under the scrutiny or input of major label oversight.

> The first time I ever saw the Butthole Surfers, Redd Kross was supporting them at The Ritz in New York in 1987. Before they played, Paul Leary came backstage and asked, "Hey, can we buy some guitar cables off you guys?" I just said, "Sure. You can borrow them. You don't have to buy them." "Oh, you're not going to want them back after we're done with them." So, they started their set, and on the very first song, Paul and Pinkus destroyed their guitars, which I thought was pretty impressive considering most bands wait until the last song to do that. —Steven McDonald, Redd Kross[10]

After *Saloon*, they would release one more album with Capitol Records, 1996's *Electriclarryland*, and then their final (as of now) full-length record, *Weird Revolution* in 2001, a joint effort between Hollywood Records and Surfdog Records. In comparison with the other major instigators of noise rock discussed earlier, Butthole Surfers offered a sort of third path within the genre, distinct from Sonic Youth's art rock leanings and Swan's droning sledgehammer approach. The Surfers introduced psychedelic touches into the mix, along with warped takes on traditional rock elements like guitar riffs and solos. For as purposefully off-putting and downright offensive as they were, they continue to cast a large shadow over the landscape of noise rock (and beyond), as evidenced by the fact that numerous books and

---

9. Butthole Surfers, "Who Was in My Room Last Night?"
10. Tanner, *Butthole Surfers*, 149.

chapters have been written about them over the years. They're like a train wreck that you feel like you shouldn't watch, but you just can't look away:

> The Butthole Surfers were influential to our music in that they helped inspire creative risk taking and experimentation with our songwriting and recordings. This was most evident in our early work and demos where we were finding and developing our own voice. The broad spectrum of recording techniques, song arrangements, and instrument usage in their recordings and their frequently transcendent live performances encouraged us in our incorporation of noise elements, feedback, and other non-traditional song components in our studio work and live shows. They inspired confidence and the courage to take these risks within the context of our vision. —Kim Thayil, Soundgarden[11]

> They made great records and actually played in our neck of the woods! Water in the drought! They zoomed past machismo and flipped a shit-dipped bird at competitive hardcore. Nothing but victory laps. . . . I loved the free-form, smearing passion. Life has so many messy fluids and the Butthole Surfers never pretended to be polite about them. After all, punk rock was supposed to be fun! . . . They didn't make music for macho boys; they knowingly and willingly made music for freaks. Freaks of any gender combination or expression. Freaks that thought about things too hard. They were there to announce that the freaks started this business and the freaks would always be the final word. With the Butthole Surfers, the freaks and the interested could find a boundary-less, creative wonderland to get messy in. —Neko Case[12]

> From 1982 through 1987, the Butthole Surfers were absolutely, undeniably, inarguably, hands-down, flat-out, the best live band on earth. Nobody could approach how dangerous and enthralling the controlled chaos of their spectacular shows were. Live, and on record, the Buttholes' imagination was unstoppable. —David Yow, The Jesus Lizard[13]

Hearing from Yow is the perfect transition, as his band is the other crucial stepping stone we need to lay out before focusing on our key bands in the next two chapters. We will spend time later on wrestling with the

---

11. Tanner, *Butthole Surfers*, 141.
12. Tanner, *Butthole Surfers*, 285.
13. Tanner, *Butthole Surfers*, 88.

transgressive elements of noise rock, particularly as expressed by the Surfers and others. But for now, The Jesus Lizard.

This foursome formed in Austin before relocating to Chicago and setting down roots there. Vocalist David Yow and bassist David Wm. Sims first joined their creative talents in 1982 in the Austin-based band Scratch Acid, a project that had many of the hallmarks of The Jesus Lizard, even in that early form. Sims was supposed to play guitar in Scratch Acid, while Yow was initially tapped to play bass, but when the original singer was kicked out, Yow moved to vocals and Sims switched to bass. The music lurched from punk-inspired blasts of distortion to full-on noise freak-outs, while Yow's howls gave the entire affair the sense of a madman reading his manifestos to the world, whether or not the world was ready to hear them.

After Scratch Acid ran its course, leaving behind a couple of EPs and one full-length record, The Jesus Lizard formed in 1987, after guitarist Duane Denison reached out to Sims and Yow for their help in recording some of his songs. Their drummer, Mac McNeilly, joined the band once all three (Denison, Sims, and Yow) moved to Chicago and the core was complete. Their mutual friend Corey Rusk, one of the cofounders of Touch and Go Records (also based in Chicago), commented on what it was like to see The Jesus Lizard at their very first show:

> I don't think anyone was prepared for the power the Jesus Lizard displayed that night. They were a visceral, gripping live band from their very first show. A few days later, the played another phenomenal, intense set at a sweaty and very insect-infested party on the roof of Martin Atkin's apartment. After these two gigs, it was very clear to me how great the Jesus Lizard were, and I was determined to do everything we could do at Touch and Go to let the rest of the world know too![14]

If the Butthole Surfers both looked and sounded like escaped patients from a mental asylum, The Jesus Lizard appeared more "normal," dressing in standard rock attire: shirts and jeans, etc. But the second their instruments started churning and Yow's vocals hit your ears, it was clear that their intentions transcended any sort of fashion or pre-established style. On their debut EP *Pure*, the closing track is a mostly instrumental piece entitled "Happy Bunny Goes Fluff Fluff Along"[15] and it sounds like they're mining some long-forgotten crevice in the Earth that will eventually lead

---

14. Jesus Lizard, *Jesus Lizard Book*, 8.
15. Jesus Lizard, "Happy Bunny Goes Fluff Fluff Along."

to the planet's very core. It's foreboding, grinding, and humorously disconcerting, especially in juxtaposition with the silly title.

The Jesus Lizard's journey paralleled the Butthole Surfers in a couple of aspects: their shows were legendary for their intensity and David Yow's onstage antics (and offstage when crowdsurfing with the audience) and they also signed with Capitol Records in the wave of hype that surrounded the weirder fringes of rock during the mid-to-late 1990s. Yow even recounted the time that his earlier band, Scratch Acid, played a couple of shows with the Butthole Surfers:

> The next time we played, we were first on the bill, followed by Butthole Surfers, Austin legends the Big Boys, and TSOL at the Skyline in North Austin. This was a pretty big show, and I had never sung in public. I was terrified. I spent most of the day throwing up. One of us had gotten hold of a whole bunch of LSD. We gave out about eighty hits of acid before we played. Hopefully, a few of those who imbibed found it an enjoyable experience.[16]

As the band's career continued, that emphasis on a live, visceral impact in their shows became one of their hallmarks. Rob Warmowski, a Chicago-based musician and audio engineer, reflected on seeing them perform in the summer of 1990.

> During what I would come to know as "Then Comes Dudley," "One Evening," "Good Thing," and "Killer McHann," the mood and moves flipped into snarling fury and back in a way I had never heard any band manage before. Huge, yet never plodding. Mannered and precise, yet never busy. And always with that nice man in the suit [Yow] who seemed like he had something on his mind. By the time the elegiac masterwork "Pastoral" came, I was ready for anything. What I got was the unforgettable set piece of Yow reaching for a giant sea sponge soaked in what appeared to be ink. While Mac, Duane, and Sim traced the mournful musical contours of what Nelson Algren called "loving a woman with a broken nose," Yow lifted the sponge to his noggin and squeezed, sending dark rivulets of blue cascading down his face, finally ruining his duds, along with any chance I had of imagining a better band.[17]

As for what might have been going through Yow's head on any given night?

---

16. Jesus Lizard, *Jesus Lizard Book*, 29.
17. Jesus Lizard, *Jesus Lizard Book*, 52.

> The original working title of "Tight 'n' Shiny" was "Metropolis." That's how it was written on set lists for a while, but being that I had a tendency to pull my balls out and hold them glistening up to the microphone, we changed the moniker.[18]

If Yow was something of an exhibitionist while performing, the entire band made a point of making their presence memorable, no matter where they went, or who was listening. Lisa Rusk, now ex-wife of Corey, reflected on how their presence was felt in her home: "They used to practice in my basement, a dank place at best, and it was *loud*. I'd be upstairs rattling, right along with the windows. The Jesus Lizard did that—made you move like you couldn't help it. This was especially true of them live."[19]

Through it all, their commitment to their collective vision remained strong and true: rumbling, metallic bass lines, driving, pounding drums, guitar parts that both flowed along with the rhythm section and also went off on their own excursions, and those street preacher-esque vocal rants from their intense lead singer. In so doing, they carved out another branch of influence for Noise Rock. If the Butthole Surfers gave the genre a psychedelic dimension, The Jesus Lizard showed that it could be groovy, almost jazzy, and yet heavy as a concrete mixing truck. Additionally, their sphere of collaborators and creative partners in the Chicago area could merit its own book. Their first label, Touch and Go, is legendary in the noise rock and experimental scenes, with releases from heavyweights like Killdozer, the Butthole Surfers, Polvo, The Rollins Band, Don Caballero, Big Black, and Shellac. Those last two bands were formed by Steve Albini, a legendary music engineer who worked with The Jesus Lizard on their first EP and their first four full length albums. Albini's resumé, both as a musician himself and as an engineer reads like a Who's Who list of alternative and indie rock beginning in the late 1980s and into the present: Pixies, PJ Harvey, Nirvana, Jawbreaker, Melt-Banana, Superchunk, Oxbow, Will Oldham, Neurosis, Godspeed You! Black Emperor, among countless others.

In the end, The Jesus Lizard's influence on noise rock continues to this day and though the band has mostly called it quits, they have reunited sporadically for special festivals and mini-tours. Far from diminishing their legacy, these shows have only reaffirmed the special place that this band holds for their fans and those lucky enough to have witnessed them live.

---

18. Jesus Lizard, *Jesus Lizard Book*, 53.
19. Jesus Lizard, *Jesus Lizard Book*, 156.

Why Noise?

Lastly, before we dive into the specifics of Oxbow, God Bullies, and others, we need to spend some time unpacking the particulars of the "noise" in Noise Rock. What is noise doing in this equation, why does it matter that this genre incorporates so much of it, and what possibilities does it open up, both sonically and theologically?

> Noise is rarely spoken about in positive terms. It's a disruption or a nuisance. It causes chaos and breaks our thought processes. It interrupts the natural order of things. When someone says, "This isn't music, it's noise," they usually don't mean that as a positive thing. And for someone to make the distinction between "noise" and "music" generally means a lack of appreciation for that disruptive kind of chaos. But noise can be music. Noise can enhance music. And for that matter, noise can be a crucial part of finding new and unique ways in which to make musical expression.[20]

> Morgan Henderson, the Blood Brothers' soft-spoken, ruminative bassist, thinks the very term is inherently dismissive. "You might as well be saying, 'I don't understand it.' When [free-jazz pioneer] Ornette Coleman played, people were like, 'This is fucking noise.' But to him and Don Cherry and Charlie Haden and Ed Blackwell, they knew exactly what was going on. It wasn't noise to them."[21]

What is it about noise that makes it noise? How it is separate from music? Or is it separate? Or perhaps framed a bit differently, should it be separate? Noise Rock provides a space where music and noise can collide on a regular basis, and thus offers us a place where preconceived boundaries can come crashing down.

Our answers to these questions will be explored throughout the ensuing chapters, but for now, I offer a few insights from Hegarty and Greg Hainge, author of *Noise Matters: Towards an Ontology of Noise*.

> Noise is negative: it is unwanted, other not something ordered. It is negatively defined—i.e., by what it is not (not acceptable sound, not music, not valid, not a message or a meaning), but it is also a negativity.[22]

---

20. Terich, "Hold on to Your Genre."
21. Sisario, "Art of Noise."
22. Hegarty, *Noise/Music*, 5.

FROM CHAOS TO AMBIGUITY

> Noise, and the music that comes from an engagement with it, tests commonplace notions of hearing and listening, and tries to destabilize not just our expectations of content or artistic form, but how we relate to those . . .[23]

> It is undoubtedly not insignificant that noise is imbued with a particular propensity for transgressing and destabilizing fixed boundaries and that it is, more often than not, associated with the auditory sense.[24]

> If noise inhabits everything because everything is in actuality formed out of noise, then what noise ultimately points to is the relational ontology according to which the world comes to pass, the way in which there is nothing that falls outside of the event, of the realm of process.[25]

We will see (hear?) much more about noise in a bit, especially when we dive into the streams of transgressive theology and weakness theology, but for now, I would like to suggest an approach to noise that goes beyond something that Hegarty posits when he asks,

> Can music be immanent? Music cannot just be out there, as it implies human organization. But just because that has been the view does not mean it has to stay the case. It would seem that music has to at least pass through agency, if only historically, for there to be, as there is in certain forms of contemporary Japanese noise music, a sense of such an immanence.[26]

What if the music of existence has passed through agency, just not a human one? Might that give space and room for an inherent music of the world (a music of the spheres, of life itself) that has been intrinsically shaped by the Divine? This would dovetail perfectly with Hainge's assertion that noise leads us to "the relational ontology according to which the world comes to pass."[27] Could it be that the music and noise humanity creates is just picking up on that signal and boosting it to our own cultures and niches? With gratitude to my friend and fellow artist, Julia Hendrickson, for sparking this next thought, much has been made about the *Imago Dei*, the images

23. Hegarty, *Noise/Music*, 5.
24. Hainge, *Noise Matters*, 11–12.
25. Hainge, *Noise Matters*, 14.
26. Hegarty, *Noise/Music*, 6.
27. Hegarty, *Noise/Music*, 6.

that we form when we talk about God, the images that help us reflect on God in some sort of physical form.

But what of the sound of God? How might we form a framework of the *Sonus Dei*? I would like to propose that noise is an invitation into this aural space. Christians throughout the ages have referred to the Word of God as the starting point for all existence. Words have sounds and require a system of noises to be formed in such a way that they can be transmitted and handed down. What if the noises we encounter are echoes of the necessary background conditions from which the first utterance that brought everything into being emerged?

The Court Jester

To preview where my argument is headed, I would like to suggest that Noise Rock is the court jester of theology and culture. It's the fool that speaks truth and wisdom. A place for biting satire and lament. A location for the contemplation of the ugliness that surrounds all of us, that many parts of society want to sweep away and disregard. Rob Johnston shares a story of a student's experience watching David Lynch's *The Elephant Man*: "He wrote that every time he sees the scene, he realizes anew that he, like John [Merrick], is a creation of God—that in fact, as Flannery O'Connor might say, "God is found most beautifully in the 'grotesque.'" For this student, John Merrick showed him "a full humanity: in suffering, in faith, in hope, and in love."[28]

I especially appreciate how Sara B. Savage describes the power of fully embodied art and the room that it makes for both us and the presence of God. In her essay, "Through Dance: Fully Human, Fully Alive," she focuses on how the art form of dance achieves this:

> These sweating, groaning, hormone-driven bodies make an unlikely tabernacle for the divine. Yet God embraces the things we reject: our bodies, emotions, woundedness, mortality. We can glimpse Christ there, unless we are offended that God should choose to be limited by what we despise.[29]

I humbly propose that Noise Rock does something similar in the music space, by making full room for our sweating, groaning bodies, in all

---

28. Johnston, *God's Wider Presence*, 54.
29. Savage, "Through Dance," 77.

their brokenness and humanity. We heal and grow, in part, by allowing ourselves to be human, to laugh at the awkwardness of our humanity, to yell at the impossible finiteness of being confined to time and space, and the deeply maddening, quintessential human trait of sensing something beyond, something other than us, something right around the corner of our mental capacity that we can't quite articulate. By diving headlong into our limitations, it frees us to live in the full light of those limitations. Furthermore, and lastly (for now), I assert that Noise Rock, by way of the visceral and instinctual ways in which it works, sometimes tiptoeing, sometimes bludgeoningly, lurches into the space of the mystic, as described by John D. Caputo:

> I am pointing to the profound resources of the mystical tradition which has learned how not to speak by speaking, to advance while erasing its own tracks, to twist and turn language so as to expose the ruptures and omissions and distortions that inhere in everything we say when we approach matters so deep. The mystics are the most profound of God's fools.[30]

If Noise Rock is the space of court jesters, the fools of the heavy music world, perhaps it is also the place of the mystics . . . stumbling with sounds and noises that are both contradictory and confounding, pointing drunkenly to a Divine Presence that is also confounding, frustrating, and yet somehow welcoming. We shall see . . .

---

30. Caputo, *Folly of God*, 12.

Chapter 4

Confusing Talk of Love with Love Itself

OXBOW

PLAYLIST:

"A Cold and Well-Lit Place"—Oxbow
"A Gentleman's Gentleman"—Oxbow
"The Upper"—Oxbow
"Letter of Note"—Oxbow
"Shine [Glimmer]"—Oxbow
"Jesus with a Cock"—Buñuel
"Other People"—Oxbow
"Frank's Frolic"—Oxbow

Scan for Playlist

The best noise rock confounds the beholder, the listener, the watcher. It confronts and annoys. It pokes, it prods, it scratches at the brain like a restless insect of an idea, skittering here and there, building in intensity until it breaks free and the concepts that we thought were fenced in and safe escape with it and pour out of our collective unconscious until we can't dismiss the new possibilities anymore.

The best noise rock ruins our hearts and forces us to bleed and rebuild, stitch up a hundred cuts, pummels us and our organs into new shapes. Forces us to abandon ports of safety and set sail for horizons unseen, even if we might head straight over the edge of the world. Like Reepicheep heading for the End of the World, this sort of art offers life anew or possible death, but not much in between. After all, "it's only after we've lost everything that we're free to do anything" (thanks Tyler Durden/Brad Pitt).

The best noise rock includes Oxbow. Formed over thirty years ago in San Francisco, this band of four individuals has simultaneously gelled and pulled apart, pursuing a vision of music that confounds, ruins, and confront. They are rock, noise, punk, chamber music, integrating elements of these genres and also somehow moving beyond them. It's a soundtrack of the future, made by outsiders who might not even be welcome in the world that they're envisioning. Oxbow is bassist Dan Adams, drummer Greg Davis, vocalist Eugene Robinson, and guitarist Niko Wenner. Over the course of their collective career, they've released seven full length albums, a couple of EPs, and a few compilations, live albums, splits, and music videos. Seven records in thirty years doesn't seem like much, especially since there was a ten-year gap between their most recent, *Thin Black Duke* in 2017 and the previous, *The Narcotic Story* in 2007.

Oxbow, *The Narcotic Story* (2007)

But what they might lack in frequency, they more than make up for in impact: their albums are intense affairs, practically forcing the hearer to actively engage in what's hitting the eardrums. To participate with Oxbow in their art requires us to shift from simply being hearers of the music over to being listeners. It's that difference between being in a conversation and absentmindedly nodding your head periodically and saying "yep" in mock agreement and actually knowing the words and ideas that are being communicated. And even then, sometimes this isn't quite enough for communing with Oxbow. Their collision of styles means that the intensity of a song will sometimes drop out just as it feels like it should be exploding. Or there's a swing in their step that wouldn't feel out of place in a 1950s musical, as "A Cold and Well-Lit Place" demonstrates. Or the track will proceed exactly as you expected (maybe even hoped?) and it is an aural battering ram that lasts as long on its own as some band's entire albums. "Shine [Glimmer]" off *An Evil Heat* is 32 minutes and 37 seconds, putting its runtime in similar territory as each of The Beatles first seven records (30–35 minutes apiece). This track builds on a foundation of drums and bass, rumbles and stretches, drones on and on. It's both contemplative and meditative, entering your mindset as confrontation, lulls you into a sense of security and then pulls you back out again, wondering what exactly you've just experienced.

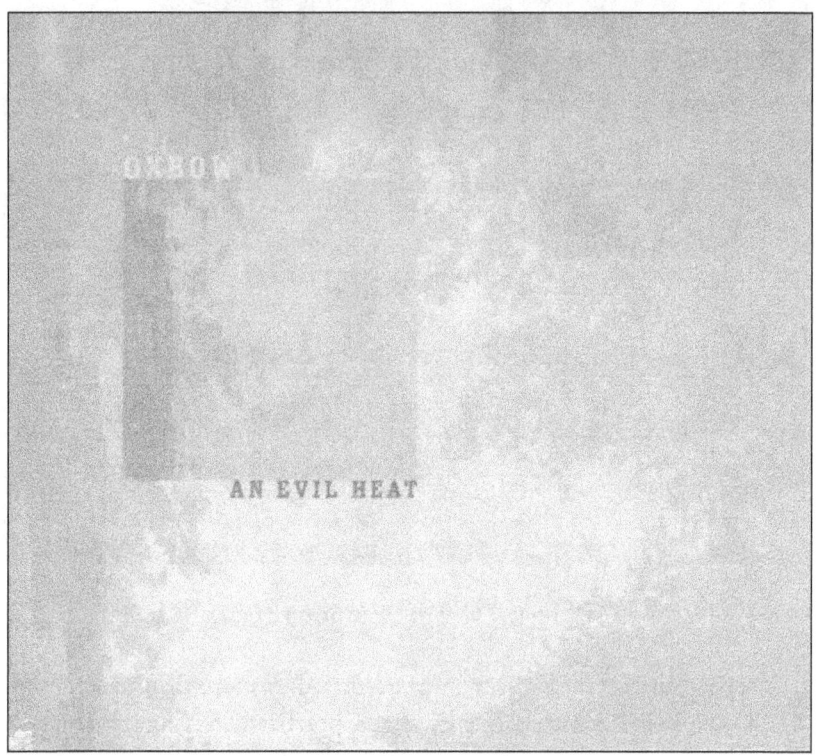

Oxbow, *An Evil Heat* (2002)

Oxbow embodies these contradictions and deconstructions all the way down: certainly musically, as we've already discussed. But their dismantling of false dichotomies and binaries extends to their lyrics and vocals as well. And it's here that we dive into the persona of Eugene Robinson himself. Robinson, a black man in his early sixties, is a singular individual onstage. He frequently dresses sharply, wearing a suit and tie (sometimes complete with a vest), and yet also tapes over his battle-worn ears in order to keep his in-ear monitors in place. His ears have sustained damage over the years due to the fact that Robinson is also a trained MMA fighter. He's been known to choke out particularly aggressive fans who are hellbent on confronting him at Oxbow shows, even though that's not his overriding approach to his stage presence. His arms and torso are covered in tattoos, though when he's wearing that suit, you'd never know it. As Oxbow progresses through their setlist, Robinson is also famous for removing his clothing, bit by bit. Not so much as a striptease, but almost as if he's shedding layers of skin, removing barriers of understanding, and remaining as an almost nude reminder of what we all are: humans, flesh and bone.

Robinson is also an author, having written several books including *Fight: Everything You Ever Wanted to Know About Ass-Kicking but Were Afraid You'd Get Your Ass Kicked for Asking*, about the world of fighting and hand-to-hand combat, *A Long Slow Screw*, a crime novel set in NYC (where he grew up) in the 1970s, and his memoir, *A Walk Across Dirty Water and Straight Into Murderer's Row*. He's also a regular contributor to *OZY.com*, where he's written pieces on a myriad of topics, including Albanian singers,[1] OJ Simpson,[2] John Wayne Gacy,[3] sex workers,[4] Rodney King,[5] and much more. In other words, Robinson is a man who's seen a thing or two in his lifetime and who appears committed to living a life packed with intersections, questions, and deep human interactions. If there's a public, living embodiment of the contradictions and confrontations offered up by the art and music of Oxbow itself, then it has to be Robinson himself.

It should come as no surprise then that these elements bleed over with full force into the lyrics of the band. While we've touched briefly on a few of their pieces thus far, at this point, we're going to dive headfirst into the ideas expressed in their most recent album, *Thin Black Duke*.

1. Robinson, "When Albanian Singers Crushed The World."
2. Robinson, "Complicated Case for and Against OJ."
3. Robinson, "Grisly John Wayne Gacy."
4. Robinson, "When Sex Workers Were Hookers."
5. Robinson, "When What Happened to Rodney King."

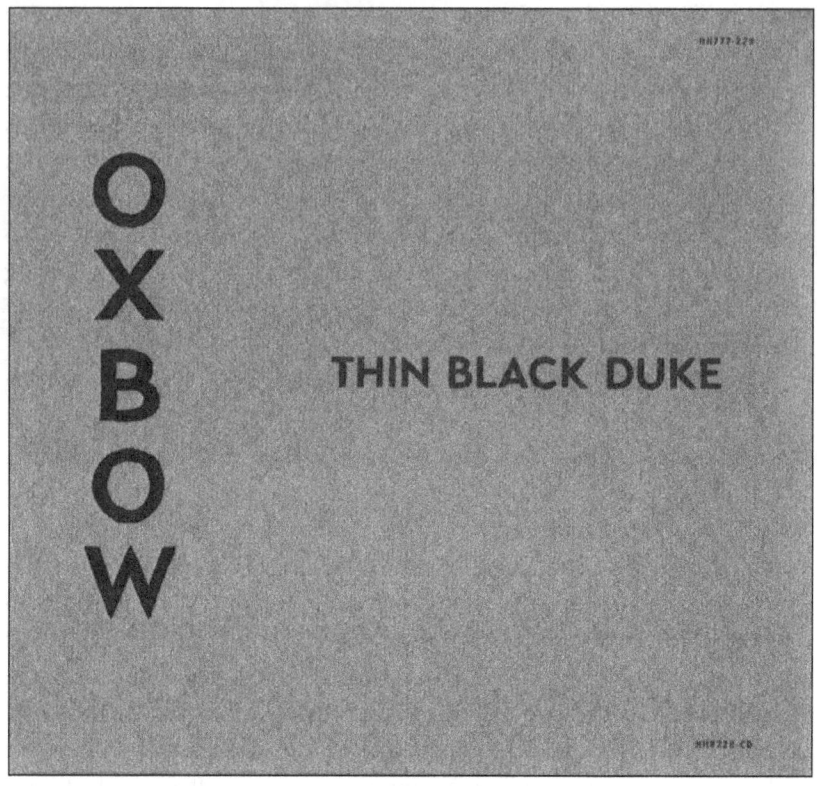

Oxbow, *Thin Black Duke* (2017)

The title itself is an obvious tribute or head-nod to one of David Bowie's more controversial characters, the Thin White Duke, and an era of his career marked (depending on who you're asking) by misunderstood critiques of Nazis and fascism, or by ill-conceived references to the same in the name of exploratory art. Similar to Bowie's creation, Oxbow's Thin Black Duke is hellbent on questioning norms, boundaries, societal expectations, and more. Thankfully, Oxbow made the decision to release a companion book to Thin Black Duke, appropriately entitled, Thin Black Book. While experimental bands like Oxbow don't always pull back the curtain on either the writing process of the music or the concepts and philosophies that inform their lyrics, Thin Black Book provides us with a rather unique deep dive into both. The interpretation of the album itself by the listener is still open-ended and needed, but the companion book gives us a bit more of a foundation on which to build our ideas. Robinson himself wrote and edited most of it. And he starts the book with a long address about the nature of the Duke. It's one that will frame where we go from here, so I present a portion of it now to you:

> The THIN BLACK DUKE is, in my mind, about the places where all that glitters IS gold, and evil is a quaint concept born of an outmoded moral framework in a place that is shorn of morality and that framework.
>
> So lucre is not really the issue. It's an abstract concept. But it's how you interpret that concept that makes the difference. And like when G-d gathers his sons and asks them what they've been doing, and Lucifer says, "walking up and down, to and fro" and you imagine him doing what he did for reasons occult to us but very clear to him: wanting us to degrade because we were meant to degrade. Fundamentally, the best kind of repudiation. I mean in the Book of Job the purpose was not to see if Job turned against G-d. That interpretation is for suckers. The point was for Lucifer to spoon feed him shit.
>
> Realizing this at the end of THE NARCOTIC STORY our narrator both surrenders and gives up. But nature/earth bound forces abhor a vacuum. So what rushed in? This impulse to tear yourself, both quietly and completely, apart. Or to quote Kierkegaard: unto death.
>
> There is a very real death at the end of the THIN BLACK DUKE. Which is to say, we won't get better. We won't get worse. We won't get anything. We won't get anywhere. Not alive. Not dead. Shorn of moral agency we're just where The Duke wants us. A perfect time for what precisely he has in mind for us.
>
> Someone once said to me as a way to mitigate the darkness, "Well at least you're not dead!" and my response was, "You don't know that."
>
> The THIN BLACK DUKE world? Of brushed gold-plated lighters, and plush carpets and mammon, mammon, mammon? Of killing luxury and the serving of human and the poisons of humans? Yes, this is all about creating a space where this happens to YOU: moral death and actual nothingness. And it's all perfumed and perfectly executed and you'll breath deeply because you have no choice.[6]

---

6. Robinson, *Thin Black Book*, 6.

Oxbow, *Thin Black Book* (2017)

This description seems to have it all: a world where the best of what humanity has to offer itself lives hand-in-hand with the knowledge that it will all fade away immediately. A world where there is some knowledge of God and/or ancient texts with stories to tell and morals to teach us, and yet those morals have become completely unmoored (or have died), no anchors left to keep our philosophical ships from drifting out to sea and never being found again. There are Biblical references to "mammon" but do such terms have any meaning remaining in the absence of agency or a framework for judging good from evil? And what of this notion that we have no choice? What could that possibly hold for us in our current stage of existence?

There's a lot to unpack here, so let's try to do so with the help of few different interpretative lenses. First, consider the overall perspective that Robinson seems to be appealing to "an outmoded moral framework in a place that is shorn of morality and that framework." He is, in essence, calling upon the post-secular existence in which we live. It is the era of "the death of the death of God," to borrow a phrase and idea from Callaway and Taylor.[7] It is a "post-traumatic" world, where some of the casualties include our faith, our morals, and perhaps even a sense of destiny and purpose.[8] It is a life lived in the full presence of the catastrophic.[9] If not even death or luxury that kills offers a way out, it is truly a philosophical outlook that seems to offer very little hope or light at the end of the tunnel . . . if indeed it is a tunnel. Perhaps we are simply doomed to live a buried existence, far longer than just three days and then resurrection.

In the light of these realizations, the Duke seems to offer a rather nihilistic spin on Ecclesiastes:

> "Now I didn't bring these drinks for nothing"
> The Duke not disheveled or dissembled says
> "And not drinking is a sin
> That offends the eye of your lonesome
> So let's tip the goddamned glass
> And get to enjoying ourselves, fast."
> Cigarettes smoke gray and blue rings
> And no one here is broke. No, no one here has anything to fear
> And while they say that the best things in life are free
> Everything around here comes with a fee.[10]

In this modern parable, everyone can afford what the Duke is selling. He is well-put together, offering those age-old temptations, alcohol and cigarettes. And why not? To not partake would be a sin. The participants here appear to have drunk fully from the knowledge of the tree and

---

7. Callaway and Taylor, *Aesthetics of Atheism*, 14.
8. Callaway and Taylor, *Aesthetics of Atheism*, 263.
9. Callaway and Taylor, *Aesthetics of Atheism*, 14.
10. Oxbow, "Cold and Well-Lit Place."

in the light of what that knowledge has wrought, they opt for what's right in front of them.

And what is this knowledge that has unwoven our existence? There is something about the Duke that seems to hint at something inhuman, something other that is just beyond our grasp. He is described in the following ways:

> You see there is some talk of his teeth being cut from ivory
> Or something else thick from below the deep
> There is some loose talk about from where the glow seeps
> That shines in his eyes.[11]

Those teeth show up again later in the album, combined with a further description of the skin:

> And teeth?
> Perfect
> And skin?
> Like some great shining alabaster monument
> To cause
> And what it affects
> There is no stink of human here
> Heavenly host with the most
> Just not this
> And toying with the toys
> You have very little choice.[12]

There's a suggestion that perhaps the Duke is of the heavenly realms, yet his manner and temptations would seem to suggest an origin outside of that mythic place. Additionally, his toying with our toys hints at a level of disinterest towards us that is unnerving. In this, I think we can see some parallels between the Duke and what some authors and philosophers refer to as cosmic pessimism: the understanding that, on some basic, almost primal state, the universe doesn't care about us. It moves and has its being with us present, but it could just as easily do the same without us.

---

11. Oxbow, "Gentleman's Gentleman."
12. Oxbow, "Upper."

This second interpretive lens comes to us by way of Eugene Thacker. He explores these ideas in his book, *In the Dust of this Planet*. Thacker highlights three key definitions of the world, of existence at large:

World—the world-for-us

Earth—the world-in-itself

Planet—the world-without-us

In essence, we live and move and have our being in the world-for-us. This is our main frame of reference and the space where humanity is central. The world-in-itself is less so, but it's still a presence that we can engage with: what we tend to call nature and the study of nature: animals, plants, minerals, the various earth sciences, etc.

In contrast, the world-without-us is largely unknowable. It's a plane of existence (with its implied knowledge) that operates without us and essentially doesn't care that we exist. It's the cold of the cosmos, the presence of nature that disrupts and destroys human life (and indeed animal and plant life) in completely amoral, disconnected ways: floods, fires, tsunamis, extreme heat, freezing cold. This is the sort of thing that we attempt to label or frame as "acts of God" or "acts of nature" or "freak accidents." But I would argue that this is, on a somewhat routine, human-sized level, a glimpse at the unknowability that Thacker is getting at in his text:

> To say that the world-without-us is antagonistic to the human is to attempt to put things in human terms, in the terms of the world-for-us. To say that the world-without-us is neutral with respect to the human, is to attempt to put things in the terms of the world-in-itself. The world-without-us lies somewhere in between, in a nebulous zone that is at once impersonal and horrific. The world-without-us is as much a cultural concept as it is a scientific one, and, as this book attempts to show, it is in the genres of supernatural horror and science fiction that we most frequently find attempts to think about, and to confront the difficult thought of, the world-without-us.[13]

What if the Duke of Oxbow's story represents this world-without-us? The character is somewhat humanized by being depicted in human form, yet there are too many details to ignore that suggest the Duke is something

---

13. Thacker, *In the Dust of This Planet*, 5–6.

other than human (a glow seeping behind the eyes, perfect teeth and skin). Thacker continues:

> I would propose that horror be understood not as dealing with human fear in a human world (the world-for-us), but that horror be understood as being about the limits of the human as it confronts a world that is not just a World, and not just the Earth, a but also a Planet (the world-without-us). This also means that horror is not simply about fear, but instead about the enigmatic thought of the unknown. . . . Horror is about the paradoxical thought of the unthinkable. In so far as it deals with this limit of thought, encapsulated in the phrase of the world-without-us, horror is "philosophical." But in so far as it evokes the world-without-us as a limit, it is a "negative philosophy" (akin to negative theology, but in the absence of God).[14]

I would humbly argue that it's the unknowability and impersonal of the world-without-us that makes it horrific. It would seem that our natural state as humans is to seek to understand what we do not already comprehend, to give things a frame within which we can grapple and wrestle with them on our terms, not theirs. And this is where successful expressions of horror of various forms can take root and grow. It's what makes the Duke both horrifying and alluring. It's not uncommon for horror stories to have a character or two who are drawn to the unknown horrific as moths to light. It's a veritable staple of the Alien series, where the spread of the xenomorphs hinges almost entirely on the willingness of an intrigued complicit party, whether it's an individual working for Weyland-Yutani or the "Company" itself as a whole. The horrific in this sense is like a siren, luring humanity to its doom.

What are we to ultimately make of these expressions? What can we glean from the Duke and his wares? I think they can provide us with a means of staring/screaming into the abyss without going blind or insane. We will all eventually have to face some form of catastrophe (if we haven't already). When we do, it will often not be a matter of making sense of it, but rather living in and through it. I think cosmic pessimism and other expressions of the horrific give us an opportunity to experience that journey vicariously through art. Grappling with the Duke via Oxbow gives us a fighting chance when we encounter him in real life.

---

14. Thacker, *In the Dust of This Planet*, 8–9.

Additionally, for those of us who lay claim to some sort of a faith tradition, the horror of the world-without-us offers a means of coming back to and rediscovering our sacred texts, which by our own admission, come from outside our world, beyond our finite frame and working through them in a way that allows us to make room for expressions and contradictions that seem impossible to hold within the human mindset. For instance, if Christians mean what they say about the Bible when they talk about it being "God-breathed," then they're saying that somehow the finite has collided with the infinite (multiple times) and that they're essentially trying to make sense of the unknowable. Encounters with God are a form of cosmic terror, to use the language of the horror genre. Perhaps this can help us move beyond the human need to parse and understand and into a sort of acceptance, a tenuous balance between the world-for-us and the world-without-us?

For our next lens, let us step outside the world of the Duke and the album and quickly take stock of what music in general can accomplish when it transcends or transgresses certain boundaries. If we're living in a world where our assumptions about the framework of that world are no longer safe (or at least bound up in centuries of supposed philosophical constructs), then we need to be cognizant of how music could help us navigate a road with no signposts, no borders, maybe even a road where there is no road.

This is a world where traditional art critique has shifted from qualitative judgments about high and low art to a somewhat more level playing field where lines are blurred. An artist like Shepard Fairey, initially famous for his street art/graffiti-inspired visual of "Andre the Giant has a Posse," has reached a level of worldwide renown and success that most working creatives would love to achieve. His most famous work might be the HOPE poster he created for Barack Obama's run for President in 2008, but Fairey's art has been used for album covers, commissioned city murals, adapted into a clothing line, and much, much more. In this way, Fairey illustrates what Christopher Partridge is arguing for in his book, *The Lyre of Orpheus*. Partridge makes the case that, while we can continue to judge the merits of certain art within the boundaries of its own form, it's almost impossible (or at least, ill-advised) to try to compare works that traditionally fall along the high/low (or pop) art divides:

> Once this ideological process is understood, it is difficult to see how one can insist on an absolute, objective difference between

> "high" culture and popular culture, between Beethoven and The Beatles. It is, again, largely a matter of taste. Of course, this is not to say that everything is of equal value and that we cannot argue that one album by The Rolling Stones is better than another . . . but rather the argument is simply that the same fundamental processes are taking place when I choose to read a graphic novel and listen to The Stooges as when I "value" a symphony by Edward Elgar or a painting by Mark Rothko. Cultural texts are not the source of value, as Johnson would maintain of classical compositions, but rather sites where value is constructed.[15]

With this central argument made, Partridge then turns his attention to certain forms of music that have been traditionally maligned. This is where his understanding of transgression and the boundaries of the sacred are vitally important. In essence, he moves the conversation into the spiritual realm by suggesting that heavy music, even if transgressive, serves multiple key purposes, all of which makes it deeply needed for the human experience.

> The boundary lines protected by religions and by the cultures they have shaped (and again, I am thinking here particularly of Christianity and Western culture, although the net could be cast far more widely) serve, not only to structure life, but to dichotomize it, to dissect it into binary oppositions: sacred—profane; pollution—cleanliness; good—evil; sanity—madness; high—low; normal—deviant; saved—damned. Such boundary marking leaves few gray areas.[16]

These are the boundary lines that we see disintegrating everywhere in our post-secular, death of the death of God life. If they're coming down in our faith discussions, if they're coming down in our films and our visual arts, why not our music as well? Partridge once again offers a defense of outsider music (punk, metal, hardcore, noise rock), by focusing on the positive outworkings of playing and listening to it:

> Numerous musicians, in pursuing a path of transgression, some bravely, some recklessly, have felt the full weight of social facts against them. This, we will see, is central to their construction as icons within a youth culture that feels alienated and disenfranchised. In standing against the flow of social facts, they have resisted the alienating, disenfranchising, and othering hegemonies of modernity. For transgressive subcultures, the popular music

---

15. Partridge, *Lyre of Orpheus*, 26–27.
16. Partridge, *Lyre of Orpheus*, 64.

icon is an Athanasius contra mundum, one who stands against the world and against social forces in the service of what might be perceived as "the sacred"—in this case freedom, autonomy, self-determination.[17]

Through this, I believe that Partridge is touching on a major component for assigning value to these genres: the willingness to be bold and to speak truth to power. There are times, in caring for the poor and the outcast, when it is absolutely necessary to stand against the cultural tides (what he refers to as "social facts"). Extending out from his reflections on high and low art, Partridge is offering up understandings of "sacred" and "profane" that are at once more fluid in one sense and yet almost more Scripturally-based in another. In lay terms, the powers that be (the Church, the State, cultural tastemakers, etc.) aren't always right and the commoner (women, minorities, the rejects, the misfits, etc.) isn't always wrong. And this is what's so compelling about Oxbow's approach.

For all the focus on the Duke in this most recent record, there are still hints of the old ways that peek through. There is still something that we can't quite get away from. It's there in the introductory text Robinson wrote for *Thin Black Book*. It's there in the title of track two on *Thin Black Duke*: "Ecce Homo." Is this meant to specifically reference Caravaggio's famous painting of Jesus on trial? At the very least, it must echo the actual trial itself, as it uses the Latin for "Behold the Man," the phrase that Pilate used when he displays Christ for the crowd before condemning him to death via crucifixion. Elsewhere, when Robinson collaborated on vocals and lyrics with Italian noise rock group Buñuel, he talked about Jesus in a confrontationally sexual way, putting the Messiah's humanity right up in our faces in a way that we rarely (if ever) see from a strictly "Christian" perspective. If Scorsese's adaptation of *The Last Temptation of Christ* brought believers out in protest at the thought that Jesus had a sexual identity, "Jesus with a Cock" would likely put them into a coma of shame and non-comprehension.

---

17. Partridge, *Lyre of Orpheus*, 66–67.

Buñuel, *A Resting Place for Strangers* **(2016)**

> And I give, I give, I give, I give
> Like Jesus
> Like Jesus
> Like Jesus
> With a cock
> Of course he had a cock
> But neutered for the age
> Deballed for the stage
> On chain, poster, and bas relief
> He's got a beef
> and the rest of us lost
> Like the weight of this goddamned cross[18]

18. Buñuel, "Jesus with a Cock."

First up, we have to acknowledge the wickedly funny wordplay that Robinson has pulled off here: "Like Jesus" is repeated three times just prior to the first mention of "a cock." While in the larger context of the song, he's obviously referring to Jesus' genitals, there's no denying that the usage of the word "cock" brings to mind the old school term used for the rooster that crowed after Peter denied Christ three times on the night of his capture.

Secondly, is it crass? Absolutely. But keep in mind what transgression can do. It can alter our perspective and give us new eyes and ears. If we live in a post-traumatic world, then surely our savior should be able to speak to that as well, right? This portrayal of Jesus forces us to face him as a human. It's easy to set him apart as a God, as a divine entity walking among us. But that also keeps him at a distance, though ironically we're told that his presence was meant to bring God closer: If you've seen me, you've seen God. And irony on irony, Robinson here is suggesting that by "neutering" Jesus, we've lessened his impact and weight. Without his full humanity, he's easier to put on a necklace, in visual art, and sculptures. Without his genitals, he is removed from us . . . and we remain lost.

Which leads to our second-to-last lens: black artistic and faith traditions. While white Christians in the US have tended to lead bifurcated lives, with norms such as secular and sacred to help divide things up and cordon off that which is unclean from that which is clean, theologian and author Josef Sorett suggests in *Spirit in the Dark* that the black experience in America has been profoundly different. As Dr. James Cone argued in *The Spirituals and the Blues*:

> Africans viewed life as a *whole* and did not make the distinctions between the "secular" and the "sacred" that are found in Western culture. . . . They combined their African heritage with the Christian gospel and reinterpreted white distortions of the gospel in the light of oppressed people striving for a historical liberation.[19]

Interestingly enough, that refusal to draw up dichotomies where they were not needed extended to the identity of Christ as portrayed in spirituals:

> Jesus was not the subject of theological questioning. He was perceived in the reality of the black experience, and black slaves affirmed both his *divinity* and *humanity* without debating the philosophical question, "How can God become human being?"[20]

---

19. Cone, *Spirituals and the Blues*, 39.
20. Cone, *Spirituals and the Blues*, 43.

Sorett explores this notion in-depth via the writings of actor, activist, and poet Amiri Baraka (born LeRoi Jones). Baraka fought for the need and ability for black artists to fully embrace and express themselves in forms that are quintessentially African-American.

> We wanted an art that was revolutionary. We wanted a Malcolm art, a by-any-means-necessary poetry. A Ballot or Bullet verse. We wanted, ultimately, to create a poetry, a literature, a dance, a theater, a painting, that would help bring revolution.... That was what it all was about. That's what the whole movement and essence of the Black Arts was raised and forwarded by, the desire by Black youth to make revolution in the US.[21]

As Sorett explains, Baraka envisioned an overarching categorization of black music that could encompass

> popular rhythm and blues, soul music, and avant-garde jazz. He referred to the last genre as the "New Black Music" and included as its practitioners musicians such as John Coltrane, Archie Shepp, and Sun-Ra. His central claim was that the blues best embodied black experience.... The blues, for Baraka, constituted a "central body of cultural experience" across time and space.[22]

Not only that, but black music for Baraka was a place where true, authentic blackness could be expressed in ways that crossed all boundaries, place, or location:

> Where some cast the blues as a secular (and profane) tradition running parallel to the (sacred) spirituals, for Baraka both were religious, inseparable, and of a kind. That is, religion was the essential ingredient in both the roots of the blues and the routes this tradition continued to travel.[23]

Baraka saw no such dividing line: "A historical teleology—from African origins through the bowels of black Christian churches and beyond—organized Baraka's interpretation of the significance of religion to contemporary black music."[24]

---

21. Sorett, *Spirit in the Dark*, 167.
22. Sorett, *Spirit in the Dark*, 180–81.
23. Sorett, *Spirit in the Dark*, 181.
24. Sorett, *Spirit in the Dark*, 182.

Baraka saw and heard within the work of "New Black musicians" a form of lament that both mourned the wounds of hatred while also providing a vision of what could be through God.

> Their hearts had been broken, Baraka suggested, by a nation-state that aligned itself with white supremacy. They sang and played out of pain caused by the continued social and political exclusion of black people in the United States. For these artists, "to play strong would be the cry and the worshipful purpose of life . . . a way into God. The absolute open expression of everything."[25]

In another potent indictment, Baraka suggested that as "Americanization and secularization came together in the 1960s . . . the 'church continues, but not the devotion.'"[26]

> Drawing clear lines between content and form, Amiri Baraka privileged the latter (spiritual/black forms) over the former (Christian/white content). In doing so, he highlighted the contributions that black people made both to American Christianity and jazz music. Moreover, in making this distinction he identified in black music a unique religious tradition that neither began nor ended with Western Christianity or the United States.[27]

Through all of these stories and these frameworks of dealing with both faith and artistic expression, I am struck by the utter perseverance of black communities within the US. Whether explicitly claimed or implicitly handed down via traditions and cultural practices, the faith that they held onto (and that held onto them) sustained them in their darkest circumstances. Interwoven with the very art that they were creating, it provided hope and light in the midst of those sufferings. Even in settings where certain black leaders felt compelled to distance themselves from an explicitly Christian tradition due to its complicity with the stronghold of white power and supremacy, they still couldn't entirely escape its mental and spiritual frameworks and structures.

> The paradox of the existence of slavery and segregation in the heart of the land of freedom had nurtured a people who embodied the American experiment. In the blues, one found the paradigmatic example of the paradox, irony, and experimentation that defined

---

25. Sorett, *Spirit in the Dark*, 182–83.
26. Sorett, *Spirit in the Dark*, 182.
27. Sorett, *Spirit in the Dark*, 183.

democracy. Irreducible exclusively to race, the blues was "the very stuff of the human condition."[28]

Somehow, their faith and the collective expressions of that faith within their communities managed to find a way forward.

While I want to be careful about assigning specific motives to Robinson and the rest of Oxbow, I do think we can utilize a similar no-holds barred, tear down all barriers approach to their art. While it's likely not explicitly faith-based or tied to one particular religious tradition over another, the way they craft their music and the way that Robinson writes his lyrics would seem to reveal a certain porousness wherein ideas that are often held at arms-length from each other are allowed to collide and breathe the same air.

What if what we're seeing in Western, American culture is the breakdown of philosophical, religious, and ideological boundaries that were never meant to be there in the first place? This leads me to the one of the most profound things that I believe music can do in, through, and for us: it circumvents our mental fences and guides us to places we might not ever reach through any other means.

> But my preoccupations these days have gotten heavy with heavy ... and are all about both surrendering and giving up and divorced from a religious concept, it's not nearly so nice and neat and not even leavened by any sort of healthy self-abnegation. It's all about the last chapters of Dante's *Inferno*. Or something like that.[29]

For my final interpretative lens, I want to take a hint from Robinson and cast our gaze (and our listening ears) back to The Divine Comedy. Dante's era was certainly different from our own in a myriad of ways, not the least of which was the weight and authority that Europe still gave to faith and Christianity in particular. Yet I think that there are parallels with the use of sound and music within the Comedy that are echoed in my basic argument here: Music gives us a means of orientation and maybe even faith when all else in our lives has been obscured and torn down.

I believe that Dante's use of auditory cues in the *Inferno* (and elsewhere throughout the entire Comedy) demonstrate an acute awareness of how sound can help orient the reader and heighten the tension and increase the sense of unease within the text. Furthermore, as the descent into hell

28. Sorett, *Spirit in the Dark*, 212.
29. Robinson, "Interview."

continues, Dante the pilgrim (as a character within the story) and his guide Virgil encounter numerous visions that are spectacularly disturbing and bizarre. Humans are contorted into inhumane shapes, tortured in varying degrees of severity. One wonders if, over time, our guides (and by extension, ourselves as readers) might become inured to their sufferings, if not for the periodic audio reminders that these are indeed human voices and human gruntings and human cries that we are hearing.

In this manner, sound in the *Inferno* orients us towards human suffering. The "instruments" and guttural/corporeal sounds of the *Inferno* are absolutely crucial to a proper framing of the entire venture. Oliver Davies explains:

> The first place in the *Commedia* at which language as human communication comes strikingly into view in all its materiality is in canto 3 of the *Inferno* (where the uncommitted and pusillanimous are). The sounds of Hell that meet the pilgrim's ears include [sighings and complaints and howlings].[30]

Mary Ann Roglieri takes it a step further. Whatever musicality might be contained within the sounds of the *Inferno*, it is "not carefully considered and worked on over time; instead it represents the souls' instant reaction to their pain and suffering."[31]

With this in mind, it's not accidental that several of the passages from this Canto seem to suggest that sound offers guidance for both Dante and the reader:

> So I moved through the bitter, filthy air,
> while listening to my guide, who kept repeating:
> "Take care that you are not cut off from me."
> But I heard voices, and each seemed to pray
> unto the Lamb of God, who takes away
> our sins, for peace and mercy. "*Agnus Dei*"
> was sung repeatedly as their exordium,
> words sung in such a way—in unison—
> that fullest concord seemed to be among them. (XVI, 13–21)[32]

---

30. Davies, "Dante's *Commedia*," 166.
31. Roglieri, "Twentieth-Century Musical Interpretations," 156.
32. Dante Alighieri, *Divine Comedy*, 288.

In this instance, the sound operates on a literal and figurative level, providing both a sense of direction in the "filthy air" and a portrayal of community. It's encouraging to hear a sense of unity in this description, even in the midst of people asking for mercy. And then once more, just a few lines later in the same canto:

> "I'll follow you as far as I'm allowed,"
> he answered, "and if smoke won't let us see,
> hearing will serve instead to keep us linked." (XVI, 34–36)[33]

This serves to reaffirm and solidify what's just come before: Sound is a connective tissue, providing the sojourners with direction when their other key sense for way-finding (sight) is hampered. In contrast with the previous example from the *Inferno*, the voices (of Virgil and the singers) offer real directionality for Dante-pilgrim. The voices that reach him before entering hell orient him emotionally and perhaps even psychologically. Here, they serve to orient him physically. Without them, he and Virgil would both be lost, left to wander and struggle in the *Purgatorio*. As it is however, Canto XVI ends with light breaking through: "You see the rays that penetrate the smoke already whitening."[34] The action of coming out of the smoke and vapors in this Canto continues into the opening lines of the next canto, as Dante-pilgrim and Virgil finally emerge from the environment-induced blindness.

It is here that we encounter perhaps the most profound use of sound in the entire Divine Comedy. While Dante-pilgrim has been struggling to see properly in the *Paradiso*, it's only after his experience of having his sight taken and navigating through speech and music that he is able to see more clearly. The spiritual orienting nature of sound restores his physical ability. Indeed, sound not only restores it, it more fully redeems his vision so that he is able to see better than he did before. The sounds of praise in paradise cut through his blindness with the suddenness of someone waking from a deep sleep into full sunlight. It's a potent description and brings the promise of the orienting nature of sound to its completion.

What might our existence sound like if we tried to allow the sound, noise, and music of our lives to help shape and orient us on the three levels that it does for Dante-pilgrim? Or perhaps we would do better to ask first, "How are the sounds of my life already orientating me emotionally,

---

33. Dante Alighieri, *Divine Comedy*, 289.
34. Dante Alighieri, *Divine Comedy*, 292.

physically, and spiritually?" Are they, in the case of Dante, helping to lift his ears (and his gaze) to heaven? Or are they contorting us into less-than human shapes?

Additionally, the boundaries we have set on truth and beauty need some adjusting, based on the sonic encounters in the Divine Comedy. Not everything that is pleasing to the ear is automatically good. The horrific sounds of hell, while not an enjoyable experience, ultimately serve a helpful, instructive purpose. We have to move beyond a binary understanding of "pleasant" sounding music on one end of the spectrum or abrasive noise on the other. Not everything that sounds "bad" is wrong and not everything that sounds "good" is safe. Especially within our current context, is it a truly life-giving thing that so many of our airways are filled with pop music that's the musical equivalent of fast food? How might we better divine an approach to sonic entertainment that informs how we listen and why we listen to certain types of music? And the deeper implications of how that music orients or disorients us?

I can't make any personal claims about the voices that the men of Oxbow are listening to in their lives, but their artistic output thus far gives us a rich tapestry for exploration. They call out the indifference of this world to our existence, yet their search for meaning suggests that there must be something out there for us to hold on to. The ways in which they combine a variety of musical genres demonstrates a fearlessness about their exploration, and gives the listener the permission to be fearless as well. And Robinson's vocals run the gamut of human experience, something that people of faith who live disembodied lives desperately need the freedom and license to explore.

> And God smiles on them or at the very least
> from down here it looks like a smile
> and he looks like God.[35]

> There are some who [will] confuse talk of love
> With love
> Looking not so [carefully].[36]

---

35. Oxbow, "Letter of Note."
36. Oxbow, "Other People."

> In very real terms, while living a life populated with those I love and those that love me, there is also the very real specter of that which can't be crawled away from: bad people, bad places in space and the very real likelihood that we are them. This is not an adolescent hunger for the dramatics afforded by some sort of state-side depressions. This is a very real summation of the approaching end and the fact that we don't have clocks at home that run backward.
>
> In 1988 when I started recording drum parts for what I was calling OXBOW, drums I played, poorly, and months before I called the much more musically adept Niko Wenner in to do for music what I was doing for words I fancied this expression a suicide note that would explain everything to everyone.
>
> Almost thirty years later, still not dead, but closer yet to dying still, while it's comforting to know that I now don't want to die, it's appalling that sooner now I must.[37]

For the follower of Jesus, it might be impossible to claim the same sort of authority for the faith across disciplines and social lines that it once had . . . but maybe that's for the best. Maybe that's the environment where faith and hope have the most opportunities to grow and flourish.

---

37. Robinson, *Thin Black Book*, 6.

Chapter 5

Let's Go to Heaven in a Big Rowboat

God Bullies

PLAYLIST:

"How Many Times"—God Bullies
"Let's Go To Hell"—God Bullies
"Monster Jesus"—God Bullies
"Detain My Brain"—God Bullies
"Act of Desire"—God Bullies
"King of Sling"—God Bullies
"Neighborhood Kid"—God Bullies
"Hate"—God Bullies

Scan for Playlist

God Bullies was a noise rock band from the Kalamazoo area of Michigan. They formed in 1986, broke up in 1995, and then regrouped in the 2000s for a few reunion shows and festival appearances. The core of their band was/is made up of Mike Hard (vocals and lyrics), David B. Livingstone (guitar, synth, samples, tapes), Adam Berg (drums and percussion), and Mike Corso (bass, organ). Other members of the band at various points included Tommy Shannon, Eric Polcyn, Tony Oliveri, and Brian Downey. During their initial run in the 1980s and 1990s, they released four full-length albums, an EP, and multiple singles. After the band broke up, several members continued making music in other spin-off projects, including Thrall and Th3y N3v3r Sl33p. While there are sonic and thematic overlaps with those bands, for the purposes of this chapter, we will stick with God Bullies' creative output.

God Bullies, *Dog Show* (1990)

From the beginning, God Bullies used religious imagery and symbolism, in a heavy-handed manner, like auditory blunt force trauma. If they had emerged during the heyday of the success of the Christian Contemporary Music genre, they would have almost certainly been confused with bands in that scene, at least based on their visuals alone. The minute some unsuspecting listener put on one of their CDs expecting the edifying sounds of Petra or maybe early Audio Adrenaline, their ears would be in for a rude awakening. Crosses are all over their artwork, from 1990's *Dog Show*, to 1992's *War On Everybody*, and even on the back cover of their final release in 1995, a seven-inch single titled *Millennium*.

God Bullies, *War on Everybody* (1992)

Five years after Andres Serrano's now-famous/infamous photo *Immersion (Piss Christ)* made waves in the art world and beyond, God Bullies used a photo of a crucifix nestled in a bed of dollar bills inside a toilet bowl as the cover of the seven-inch single, *Tell Me / Creepy People*. While it might not have had the same seismic impact as *Piss Christ*, this photo reveals a band that was fearless in confronting the commodification of the Christian faith. By diving headfirst into that imagery (and more Christian verbiage in their lyrics), I would like to suggest that they used aspects of transgressive art to upend and critique the predominant expressions of mainstream evangelical Christianity in America at that time.

God Bullies, *Tell Me/Creepy People* (1992)

To help set the stage for their music and the ways in which they pushed against the popular forms of public religion during their time as a band, consider the preeminent evangelists who were at the height of their success in the 1970s and 1980s. Jim and Tammy Faye Bakker's

TV program, *The PTL Club*, launched in 1974 and ran until 1987. Pat Robertson's show, *The 700 Club*, began in 1966 after he launched his own network (Christian Broadcasting Network) and continues into the present. Robertson also founded a private Christian school in 1977, dubbed CBN University, now renamed Regent University. Additionally Robertson even ran for political office, attempting to become the Republican Party's presidential nominee in the 1988 campaign.

1979 saw the founding of the Moral Majority, a right-wing group founded by Jerry Falwell Sr. as an attempt to merge certain conservative Christian values with the political agenda of the Republican Party. Notably, Falwell Sr. also founded Liberty University, a school that continues to have deep ties with conservative political ideologies to this day. Other prominent televangelists of this same era included Jimmy Swaggart and Oral Roberts. Swaggart's TV show, *The Jimmy Swaggart Telecast*, began in the 1970s and hit its peak in the 1980s, before sex scandals in the latter part of that decade began undercutting his influence and cultural sway. Similar to Robertson and Falwell Sr., Roberts founded his own university in Tulsa, OK, in 1963. He also had TV programs and specials that began in the mid-1950s and ran until 1980.

Of course, all of these men lived in the shadow cast by the biggest name of all, Billy Graham. Graham's approach to and use of mass media, from print to radio, TV to films, was a model for decades to come. While the assessment of his career as an evangelist has tended to garner greater respect than some of the men mentioned above, his work was not without its own share of controversies. Some of these included his first visit to Harry S. Truman, wherein he angered the president for praying publicly on the White House lawn and disclosing aspects of their chat that Truman deemed private, his recorded conversations with President Richard Nixon, and even his lack of full support for Martin Luther King Jr.'s work for greater civil rights for Black Americans.

The point in setting the table this way is to highlight the ways in which certain forms of public, conservative, and politically-involved Christianity were prominent during this time, not just in Christian circles, but across the country on a national level. This is the backdrop in which God Bullies operated, and it was these forms of Christian expression that they were interested in both parodying and critiquing. I've touched briefly on the usage of cross iconography in their art. While it's possible that a viewer/listener could interpret the crosses broadly in a myriad of ways that aren't explicitly Christian, the surrounding art as a whole helps solidify the idea that the faith tradition being examined and wrestled with is indeed the evangelical form of Christianity.

In a 2021 interview with musician and podcast host Conan Neutron, God Bullies lead singer Mike Hard reflected on how their collective setting framed who they were and what they were creating:

> Coming from the Midwest, it's the Bible Belt. We've been led astray ever since youth, you know. You're not born to hate, you know, you're not born with that feeling. So it's taught to you. Your whole life you believe everything you're taught, but then you start college town, you start reading other things and seeing other things and experiencing other things and you realize you've been lied to your whole life.[1]

As he would go on to explain in other portions of the interview (and as it becomes abundantly clear in the lyrics throughout the band's existence), much of Hard's response to his surroundings was to push back with the utmost intensity:

> We were an intense band because, you know the environment we lived in is really intense, especially in the Midwest. I started wearing the suit and tie all the time as a representation of like, this frustrated middle class working guy that finally sees he's been led astray his whole life. When you see that light and you're illuminated, it's a really intense feeling and I try to go through that gradual progression in a show where you're in a suit and tie and you look like all these other motherfuckers in a suit and tie, but you eventually see this man go totally mad when he's confronted with reality.[2]

The sound of God Bullies is that of someone being driven mad by deception and lies, yet still raging against that madness with the hope (desperation even?) that there is something more, that what's been promised is perhaps a warped version of what's actually true.

> And that's intense if you really think about it. Everything you believed and thought you believed in is totally a lie. That betrayal is, that's intense and trying to show an audience that emotion or that feeling . . . like you know, I was taught to hate you know. I was taught to believe that someone died for me, that guilt that's

1. Hard, "God Bullies."
2. Hard, "God Bullies."

associated with that, it's intense. So we try to get that out in front of people, this whole awakening thing, like being saved or being born again. All sudden, "Wow. I'm enlightened, I see the light now. I don't hate women, I don't hate black people." Once you get through that and see that light . . . I mean, look, what we're going through right now. I think it's exactly what we were talking about you know, twenty years ago.[3]

If Oxbow's approach brings to mind images of dancing with God and humanity, acknowledging the multi-faceted forms that faith, doubt, and humankind itself can embody, God Bullies lunge for the jugular with the viciousness of an attack dog and refuse to let go until the lies have all bled out. The scales have fallen from their eyes and someone is going to pay for the suffering that they and the people around them have endured. Given what we have learned about so many of the famous Christian figureheads from that era, perhaps it shouldn't be surprising that God Bullies punched back in this manner, but there is something stunning and almost breathtaking about how incisive they were in the moment. There's an almost Biblical quality to the clarity with which they issued these jeremiads. Their final full-length album, *Kill the King*, is packed with such moments:

> For crying out loud, when will it stop?
> You're only hurting yourself.
> Your crying won't help. How many times I got to tell you?
> How many times does it take?
> How many ways am I going to lose before I learn from my mistakes?
> How many times? How many men have you lied to?
> How many men do you trust?
> How many lives have been wasted on hope and faith and love?
> You tell me how many times?
> How many girls have you slept with?
> How many boys have you touched?
> How many times have you done it? How many times at once?
> How many times?
> You're only hurting yourself.[4]

---

3. Hard, "God Bullies."
4. God Bullies, "How Many Times."

Elsewhere, there's a lament of the structures and systems of power that oppress, the Church being only one of many:

> I confess my sins.
> I give up my rights.
> I deny all the charges against me.
> The cops on TV, the cops in Las Vegas,
> the cops in my home town are rich and famous.
> Watch out all you 1 percenters.
> Possession's nine tenths of the law.
> When it's too illegal to possess a weapon then it's too dangerous to disarm.
> Watch out for those Christian commies with their wallets and smart cards.
> Pick a card, any card. What's behind door number three?
> He is a blind bastard, he is a blind bastard, and he holds the key.
> It's illegal to possess a mind too dangerous to control.
> Watch out all you motherfuckers, next comes the anal probe.
> Five percent brain, one percent die.
> Take your own chances living the lie.
> What are my chances? What are your chances?
> What are my chances? What are your chances?
> Living the lie, detain my brain, detain my brain,
> cha cha cha![5]

In pushing back against these systems and expressing the deep-seated fear that comes from living under them, Hard is voicing that rebellion in a manner that will likely trip up a lot of people. His lyrics are a mix of sarcasm, anger, profanity, and social critique . . . and for some it will likely be a medicine too bitter to take. And yet, twenty-eight years later, it's tough to dismiss them. The girls and boys abused and swept under the rug? The one percenters? Powerful cops above reproach and reform? In his interview with Neutron, Hard acknowledged that much of what they talked about throughout their career was only becoming more relevant with each passing year. Even the line in "Detain My Brain" about anal probes is a reference to famous conspiracy theories about alien abduction . . . and now we can't seem to escape conspiracy theories around each corner, whether it's about the legitimacy of our elections or questioning the safety of vaccines.

5. God Bullies, "Detain My Brain."

God Bullies, *Plastic Eye Miracle* (1989)

God Bullies' visuals also included photos of baptism, communion, a Bible being opened (or possibly closed), and masses of people in their Sunday best. Their first EP, *Plastic Eye Miracle*, features a cross of thorns and three long nails, a clear reference to the suffering and crucifixion of Jesus Christ. The follow-up to this EP was a double single release, entitled *Join Satan's Army*. Almost as if they were flipping the bird and keeping folks on their toes, the cover art depicted a demonic looking Uncle Sam, complete with scaly skin, narrowed eyes that look like those of a snake, horns coming through his top hat, and a pentagram with 666 in the middle. It would be flat-out cartoonish, unless one were to know the seriousness and horror with which conservative Christians would respond to these sorts of visuals. So even when God Bullies are using "Satanic" images and concepts, they're doing so in a way that only makes complete sense in the broader evangelical sense. These are the sorts of tropes and visuals that would have led to record burnings and calls for boycotts and bans if God Bullies' popularity had grown to a wider audience, beyond the scenes that already supported punk, noise rock, and heavy rock.

God Bullies, *Join Satan's Army* (1990)

In reference to their song "The King of Sling," in which Hard sings, "They killed the man who would be king for his Rolex watch and diamond ring. They had money in one hand and a gun in the other,"[6] he suggests that his motives on-stage were geared to get people to question everything:

6. God Bullies, "King of Sling."

> I think I was more the preacher with the child in his hand . . . and we did like the baby doll thing as that type of symbolism. It was like here's this mad guy holding a baby, you know, what is he is he gonna drop it? Is he going to kiss it? Is he going to nurture it? Our shows used to be like . . . we would have pornography all over the stage and baby dolls and flowers. . . . We snuck into a cemetery and stole the plastic flowers off the heap in the back and American flags everywhere, crosses. . . . We try to wreck it, destroy it all by the end of the night. To take these icons and just totally destroy them and you know, hopefully the baby made it through the night without its body parts being torn off by the crowd.[7]

In his estimation, Hard viewed the various elements of what they had onstage (and I would contend, by extension, the rest of their visual presence in their albums) as opportunities for people to be confronted with symbols packed with meaning . . . and then to wrestle with what those symbols truly meant for them. We will explore this more later when we dive into what a theology of transgression could look like and why it's vitally important in our current day and age, but the following insights from Hard are a great primer for what's ahead:

> Symbols are symbols to different people and they represent different things and we're all about destroying all icons, destroying all symbols, and becoming a human again. So that was the process of a show: it was coming out all structured in a suit and tie with a structure all around you, holding a Bible and all this structure and then taking it all away, removing it you know and becoming naked.[8]

Their songs often musically mirrored this approach. If the symbols of crosses and images of Bibles and baptisms and the various trappings of Christianity were repeatedly revisited, almost like visual bludgeons, many of the God Bullies tracks implemented repetition to drone into your ears. It could have the effect of a sledgehammer, just pummeling away at your eardrums, or it could work almost as a hypnotic technique, drawing you in and letting part of your brain get lost in the rhythmic repetition, allowing other portions of your mind to get more engaged with what's actually being discussed. In the first song of their first album ("Act Of Desire" from *Mama Womb Womb*), they already demonstrated great skill at this approach:

7. Hard, "God Bullies."
8. Hard, "God Bullies."

> I can imagine when you put on "Act of Desire" on and you know, you have Jack Van Impe you know going on there. You know, "it's the beat, the beat, the beat of the drums, louder and faster, faster and louder," you know, and Adam's just going to it on with his tribal drum . . . yeah it sets a good kind of trance for the rest of the record.[9]

This song uses those Van Impe samples to set up an oppositional experience. On the one hand, you've got the televangelist's critiques of certain music and sounds, and on the other hand, you have the music almost directly mirroring the very elements he's criticizing: a repetitive beat that doesn't really let up throughout the duration of the song, and Hard's sole lyrics are a looped track of him almost barking out "act of desire!" Interestingly, Van Impe was also a Michigan native, having been more in Freeport, about an hour away from God Bullies' initial home base of Kalamazoo. This spiritual grift wasn't just isolated to the South after all. They knew how to parody and satirize it perfectly. In "Artificial Insemination by Aliens," they managed to both mock Christian children's programming and the Evangelical obsession with controlling sexual behavior through shame:

> How did John the Baptist die? Now that's a very good question.
> Of course it is, I know the answer to that!
> What's the answer? Now how did John the Baptist die?
> I know, I know!! Of a heart attack!
> A heart attack? No Joey, that isn't right. He got his head chopped off!
> You did *unintelligible*
> That's right. Oh now Joey, what am I going to do with you?[10]

This dialogue occurs at the start of the track, sampling what appears to be a legitimate radio play or dramatization between a couple of characters. While the sample is not credited within the liner notes of the album, the feel and sound of the recording brings to mind the puppet tapes and performances that Tammy Faye Bakker created in the early days of the Bakkers' ministry. It would not be out of place on a record like "Oops! There Comes A Smile" by Jim & Tammy & Their Friends. This intro is then perversely juxtaposed with the rest of the song, as Hard encourages the listener to celebrate and enjoy

---

9. Hard, "God Bullies."
10. God Bullies, "Artificial Insemination by Aliens."

masturbation, flying in the face of what was considered forbidden by most Christian leaders of that era (and even still by some today).

Their use of drone, repetition, and sampling would surface multiple times throughout the God Bullies' albums on tracks like "How Many Times" and "Peace And Love." From a musical genealogical perspective, God Bullies took the freak-out approach to noise rock pioneered by the Butthole Surfers and grafted into it their own sense of Detroit-inspired rock'n'roll. As Hard explained, "It was all supposed to be an out of your body experience, getting outside of your shoes and putting on someone else's feet or getting outside of your body and being able to look at yourself a little bit."[11] We've touched on embodiment a little bit thus far, but I think this is a really fascinating bit of information to engage with. He says that their music and the live experience of their performances were meant to get you out of your body, but what's interesting is that the desired result from that experience is the ability "to look at yourself" anew, with fresh eyes and understanding:

> We're gonna make you feel alive and in the room with us for these few moments we have to gather tonight. And man, those forty-five minutes you have with a crowd—or however long—those are your minutes with those people, and you want to impress them. You want to make them feel like we're all the same people, we have the same feelings, we have the same emotions, but we basically clearly we've been lied to and they've been misconstrued and they're pointed [in] opposite directions. So those few moments we have together, it's all about living in the now.[12]

---

11. Hard, "God Bullies."
12. Hard, "God Bullies."

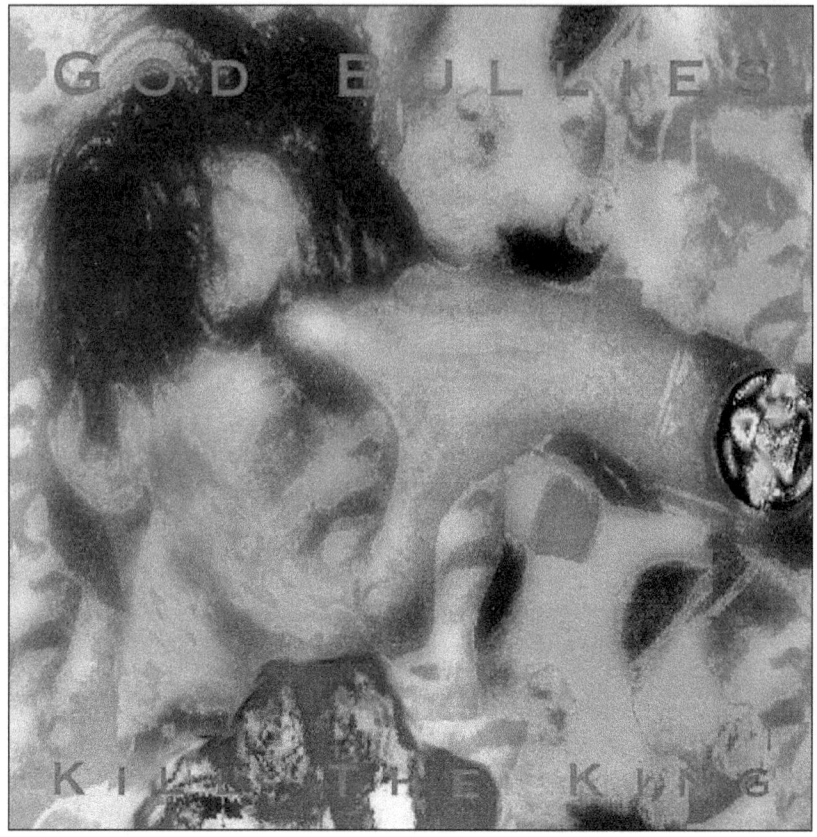

God Bullies, *Kill the King* (1994)

In their transgressive approach, I would contend that God Bullies was actually carving out space for all of us to rediscover our humanity in a fuller measure, including a bodily reminder of who we are and what we routinely sacrifice and give up in order to survive in the United States. The industrial struggles of Detroit specifically and other parts of Michigan more generally are summed up well in *Kill the King*'s opener:

> Over where the factory is, that's where you find the neighborhood kids these days. Don't know right from wrong. Their attention span is about this long.
> Forgive them, they do not know.
> They only do and say what they're told.
> Forgive them, it's not their fault.

> They're just lonely. They're just lost.
> Behind my complex there's a neighborhood bar.
> I can find what I want without looking too hard. I get drunk, I get high, but when I come down, it's the same old place.
> It's the same old town. I run, I hide, but I can't get away.
> I keep coming back to this dirty city.
> I feel lonely. I feel lost.
> I feel guilty, but it's not my fault.
> I've seen a lot and getting scared. You can call me paranoid.
> I just try to be aware.
> In those buildings, way up in the sky there's a man in an office cutting up pie.
> He's full of jealousy. He's full of greed. He'll do anything to succeed.
> Forgive him, it's not his fault.
> He's just lonely.
> He's just lost.[13]

Their setting was one of dehumanization, both through corporate mistreatment and religious manipulation, and so their art was a response to both these systems and pushback against them. Their music was a harsh critique of the working class life. And it was both genuine, filled with intent and purpose, and a performative act to get onlookers to wake up. When asked about whether the band as a whole was "as whacked out in real-life as they were on record,"[14] Amphetamine Reptile label founder Tom Hazelmeyer said, "They were definitely a collection of miscreants and oddballs. It definitely wasn't a case of putting a burning bible out on your bare chest during the set, then go to your day job as an accountant right after. Mike Hard is all you see on stage all the time, ha-ha."[15] Pair that input with the perspective of guitarist David B. Livingstone:

> And it's like, okay, yes, that's Mike Hard up there, but he has his buttoned-down suit businessman-with-a-tie persona. He's totally taking the piss and mocking just whole classes of people at once. And some of them are smart enough to figure out that they're being mocked and some of them aren't.[16]

13. God Bullies, "Neighborhood Kid."
14. Kroneiss, "Circling the Pile."
15. Kroneiss, "Circling the Pile."
16. Prindle, "David B. Livingstone."

Ultimately, I would like to suggest that what the God Bullies collective work and presence represents is a type of "deathwork." In his book *My Life Among the Deathworks: Illustrations of the Aesthetics of Authority*, sociologist Philip Rieff uses the phrase "deathwork(s)" to categorize certain works of art that take the values of a particular culture and use the representational elements of those values (words, images, etc.) to subvert and destroy them: "By deathwork I mean an all-out assault upon something vital to the established culture. Every deathwork represents an admiring final assault on the objects of its admiration: the sacred orders of which their arts are some expression in the repressive mode."[17] Rieff goes on to suggest that "the historic age of prophet and apostle has ended," and thus, "we must address the great negational theorists and artists of third world: Freud, Joyce, Duchamp (and some not as great: 2 Live Crew or Antonioni)."[18] While it appears the Rieff was able to appreciate and see the value of certain deathworks, on the whole, he viewed them as something detrimental to the culture at large:

> Deathworks . . . can be read or seen in everyday life, where they are far more fatal in their implications for not being correctly read. The unconscious art of everyday deathworks depends entirely upon the blindness of both the deathworker and those upon whom the work works.[19]

Perhaps the larger issue for Rieff was the risk that certain deathworks present when, through their subversion of core shared values and institutions, they would seem to offer a celebration of the very things they're meant to be overthrowing. In other instances, Rieff pushed back on specific deathworks in totality. In the case of Serrano's *Piss Christ*, Rieff was incapable of seeing anything of merit or sacred weight in the piece. Presumably working from a theological hermeneutic from above, wherein doctrinal propositions are given weight from a place of authority, rather than from below, in the muck and the mire of existence, he says:

> What is pleasing about this work of art? You can have a death mass that is pleasing. There is something affective in Holy Writ, in its spiritual translation as in the KJV. Piss Christ is an antisacramental image. Sacrament is a fusion with the highest and the central event in the dramaturgical enactment of highest authority. The sacrament as fusion with highest authority is inverted to the image in

17. Rieff, *My Life Among the Deathworks*, 7.
18. Rieff, *My Life Among the Deathworks*, 8.
19. Rieff, *My Life Among the Deathworks*, 8.

> Piss Christ as a fusion with the lowest. The highest is identified down in an act of incredible crudity. It amounts to an assault that lowers the Catholic identity of Galatians 2:20 to the level of excrement. Christ is in you, and so you are piss.[20]

Notably, Rieff doesn't cite the passage in Philippians 2:5–8, wherein the author of this letter says that Jesus emptied himself of his divinity and lowered himself to the existence of humanity itself. While the thought of a crucifix in a container of urine has the capacity to be shocking, perhaps we have not meditated enough on the shocking nature of the Divine opting to be born as a baby who pisses and defecates on himself and needs the help of his parents to clean his buttocks and genitals. Indeed, it is this perceived threat of lowering God, Jesus, and even Scripture itself that seems to have disturbed Rieff so much when he reflects that "contemporary translations of scripture banalize the readings and so lower the spirit, bringing the words down to contemporary readers, rather than raising them up."[21] We will return to this idea of a theology from below or a theology of weakness later, but for now, I would like to suggest that perhaps deathworks are absolutely vital for the continued life and growth of faith and cultural engagement, not in spite of, but because they emphasize that which is thought to be lowly and unbecoming.

When Mike Hard spoke of how he used the presence and image of a baby on-stage in his performances, he articulated a fear that the baby might get passed around in the crowd during a concert, and in the process, might return to the stage in literal pieces, in the event that the participants had actually pulled it apart. This immediately brings to mind another possible recent deathwork, Darren Aronofsky's *mother!*, a film that is at once both disturbing and compelling, divisive and captivating. Set within a mansion in the countryside, the mother of the film, played by Jennifer Lawrence lives in relationship with a male figure, played by Javier Bardem, named simply Him. The story itself is highly allegorical, and thus these two characters can, at different points within the tale, be interpreted as possibly Adam and Eve, the Creator and Creation, God and Mother Mary. They are meant to be symbolic of mythic concepts, larger-than-life identities, ideas that are foundational to major systems of belief and indeed even how we understand ourselves as humans.

20. Rieff, *My Life Among the Deathworks*, 98.
21. Rieff, *My Life Among the Deathworks*, 98.

Thus when there is a sequence later in the film where mother has given birth to a baby boy, we get the sense that (combined with an earlier miscarriage), this is momentous and miraculous and something to behold with wonder. Life is given a new sense of preciousness. And yet within minutes, this is shattered when Him allows a mass of people that have gathered within their home to see their son. The baby is seized by the crowd and is initially passed around by hand, until the horde becomes more and more frenzied and violent, leading to the newborn's death as they literally tear the infant limb from limb, into pieces, which then they begin to consume. The visceral nature of what we are witnessing as viewers is undeniable. It is absolutely horrific and dehumanizing. How could anyone do that to a child? How could these people be left to live in the face of such a tortuous death? Yet in keeping with the grand, sweeping gestures of the film, the literal eating of a baby, given over to the crowd in an almost sacrificial way, gives viewers who align with the Christian tradition a fresh and unsettling take on the death of the Son, one who we are called to regular remembrance through the sacrament of the Eucharist, consuming his body and blood through the bread and the wine.

By bringing this movie into conversation with both God Bullies and Rieff, I don't want to be so presumptuous as to suggest that Mike Hard's usage of a baby doll prop in their live performances was explicitly meant to encourage audiences to think about communion in a new way. But I do think that, through juxtaposition and subversion, it provided a different type of invitation to a different sort of communal table/experience, wherein shock and the profane can wake us up to truths we're inured to. It's the infamous violent grace of Flannery O'Connor's short stories, the old grandmother who would have been a good woman if someone had been there to shoot her every moment of her life.[22] But what if people misinterpret these things, as Rieff feared? What if people cling to violence as a way of life, rather than realizing that the violence is being used as a creative device to show that a different path is possible? This issue is precisely why thoughtful, nuanced, in-depth engagement with cultural traces is so desperately needed. We need to be able to wrestle with the art itself, on its own terms, as well as assessing and engaging with the artists creating it, to get a sense of who they are and the worlds that they are imagining. And while art is certainly open to various levels and angles of interpretation, hopefully we

---

22. See Flannery O'Connor's "A Good Man Is Hard to Find," in O'Connor, *Complete Stories*, 133.

can use our tools of understanding and dialogue to encourage a thoughtfulness that is ultimately life-giving, not life-taking.

We'll bring this chapter to a close with the lyrics from the final God Bullies song on their final album. "Hate" is a deathwork, bringing a myriad of identities and slurs into a churning morass of ever-building noise, chaotic guitars, and relentless drums. It is a disturbing and frightening thing to behold, a mirror held up to each of us, if we're willing to listen and gaze into the abyss that is the American identity. Some of the terms/names used feel more neutral than others: job, housewife, baker, woman, baby, human, man, brothers, sisters. And yet, within the context of the lyrics, these terms are lumped in with violence: soldier, enemy, dead hippie, butcher, bomb, weapon, rapist, pervert, narc, virus, and on and on. Christian, Jew, Arab, Baptist, Muslim, Jesus, Stalin. All is in all. There is no line here, no sacred, no profane:

> Hate is a very powerful thing. Hate is a very personal thing. Hate is a very passionate thing. Hate is a very positive thing. You are a soldier on the frontier. You must know your enemy will kill you. You are a worker in a colony. You must do your job or your government will kill you, kill you, kill you. You are a killer. You are a housewife. You are a deadhead. You are a hippie. You are a dead hippie. You are a Christian. You are a fascist. You're a dentist. You are a felon. You are a lawyer. You are a butcher. You are a baker. You are a bitch. You are a bomb. You are a woman. You are a Jew. You are a redneck. You are a loser. You are paranoid. You are a baby. You are a moron. You are a man. You are a Muslim. You are KKK. You are a wet dream. You are a bastard. You are an Arab. You are a junkie. You are Baptist. You are a mother. You are Jesus. You are Stalin. You are a drunkard. You are a human. You are a dad. You are a maggot. You are a fly. You are a fly. You are vulgar. You are dead. You are a pillow. You are an oyster. You are a rapist. You are a drainpipe. You are virus. You are a parrot. You are a weapon. You are a nigger. You are God. You are a wrestler. You are stillborn. You are stubborn. You are beheaded. You are sick. You are a penis. You are a tea cup. You are a pervert. You are a narc. You are a pig. You are my brothers. You are my sisters. I'll cut off your fingers. You are my children. I am your king. I hate you. I hate you. I hate you.[23]

By combining all of these terms, I believe that God Bullies was offering up a complex and deliberately troubling picture of human existence

---

23. God Bullies, "Hate."

in the US. There are concepts that we as a nation say that we value in this song, served up right alongside the parts of ourselves that we often want to disregard and ignore. We're left to wrestle with the perspective of the song: Who is speaking? Is it Hate itself? Is Hate driving us to do these things, to be these things, and to call each other these names? By subverting both traditional musical structures and conventional lyric approaches (verse-chorus-verse-chorus-bridge-chorus), "Hate" embodies Rieff's deathwork definition. In the parlance of *Stranger Things*, it is a hymn from the Upside Down. It sings the praises of what we should all fear becoming, and in so doing, reveals just how far down that path we've already walked. The call of this deathwork is the unspoken invitation to reject this path and carve a new one.

Chapter 6
All Roads Lead to Embodiment

PLAYLIST:

"Politicians In My Eyes"—Death

"Cheek"—The Chariot

"Death From Above"—Thrice

"The Heart of Rock 'n' Roll (Is the Profit)"—Culturcide

"Grand Island, Neb."—STNNNG

Scan for Playlist

Tucked away somewhere in the subtext of this chapter is a lame joke about three different theologians walking into a bar, accidentally bumping into each other, and then sharing a hearty laugh because they all ordered the embodiment stout, since it was the draft special of the day. And this silly riff on the bar joke trope is giving away the end right here at the beginning: while we have riffed on aspects of the following three forms of theological engagement here and there, now it's time to dive into transgression, liberation, and weakness to more fully explore how they connect with key attributes of noise rock. As we'll see by the end of this chapter, it's essentially a Venn diagram with embodiment at the center.

Transgression

We've already touched briefly on Partridge's book, *The Lyre of Orpheus: Popular Music, The Sacred, & The Profane*, in our exploration of Oxbow's work. We're going to spend more time with that text right now, as it deconstructs the long-held division between "high" and "low art," suggesting that rather than being a divide that's based on artistic merit or quality, the origin of the distinction is based in economic and political power structures. "High" art was that which was embraced by the classes in power, and "low" art (sometimes referred to as folk art) were the forms that were relegated or left over for the commoners. So rather than being a question of quantifiable "goodness" or "badness," this division was a way of playing the power game that forced people into separate groups based on nothing more than whether they were "lucky" enough to be born into the right situation or "unlucky" enough to be born into the wrong one.[1]

From here, Partridge breaks down why transgression (or the intentional crossing of human-instituted boundaries) within music is so vital and necessary. It is a means of tearing down those high vs. low art walls, and a potential pathway for folk art to be fairly seen and heard and properly assessed. The spiritual significance of this process is to make sure that we, as people who often have the ability to choose how and when we interact with music can be more informed listeners. We need to be making the time to expand our auditory horizons and not just following the recommendations of our radio stations and the tastemakers of our own communities. Voices from the margins, from the outskirts of what is popular, desperately need to be heard. Transgressing our own self-imposed

---

1. Partridge, *Lyre of Orpheus*, 24–36.

boundaries is vital. As Marsh and Roberts discuss in *Personal Jesus*, popular or "low" music can help us reflect on whether our own theological practices are too narrow. If believers are not open to God's activity outside of church life, then their faith risks becoming impoverished.

Although Partridge is not working from a framework that explicitly cites liberation theology, he does highlight how heavy music (of which noise rock is most certainly a part) allows for a form of embodiment that dovetails nicely with elements of that theological approach. He talks about how certain aspects of metal and punk allow for one to get lost in the music, overwhelmed and overtaken on a sensory level by the sounds of feedback and the roar of the amps. It's often an earthshaking experience:

> Indeed, I write this following an evening's reflection immersed in the continuous, bass-heavy, floor-shaking, surround sound, black metal thunder of a Sunn O))) concert. Following the dark ritual, I walked onto the streets of Manchester, my hearing impaired, with a sense of what I think was awe. In the Dionysian subversion of the Apollonian and the violent resistance to quotidian order, I experienced something profound. To be drawn out of everyday life and immersed in continuous, bone-shatteringly loud, dense, sonic dissonance for two hours evokes a sense of both unease and "mystical" detachment from the conditioning rationality of modernity. As we will see, the ability of popular music to do this has significance in terms of our experience of the sacred/profane.[2]

Just what is that significance that he is referring to? While his personal touchpoint here is the iconic Sunn O))) (who almost always perform dressed in black robes, like monks or ancient priests), the "sonic dissonance" discussed could just as easily refer to Swans, and their early nexus of No Wave and Noise Rock. What exactly makes heavy music so valuable? Why is it important? For those who participate in it, either as creators, participants/listeners, or both, these genres often provide a source of catharsis, an outlet for expressing emotions that are difficult to convey in any other manner. According to Steve Von Till, vocalist and guitarist for doom metal legends Neurosis, "Sometimes it feels like a war for your soul. That you have to do these things for your soul and if you didn't? Your soul is what would pay."[3] These forms of expression seem to resonate on a profound level, as evidenced by the fervent communities

---

2. Partridge, *Lyre of Orpheus*, 69–70.
3. Thomas, "Blood, Sweat, and Vinyl."

(or scenes) that come to life based either around a particular band or label, or in a certain geographical area. The instances of the latter tend to focus on key venues for live shows and/or a grouping of likeminded and like-hearted bands that form their own creative circles.[4]

All of that is well and good, and we'll return to the communal aspect in just a bit, but what about the broader spiritual implications of the ways in which heavy music tends to push the boundaries? After all, if there were no possible threat, then the critics of these genres would have little-to-no ammo for trying to marginalize or demonize it, right? If we are to mount a defense of these bands and the potent noise that they're creating, we have to identify some foundational aspects that make the case for celebrating and participating in the shape of this music. To that end, *The Lyre of Orpheus* provides us with some helpful insights. We have already alluded to Partridge's argument that the traditional divisions between high and low art are, in fact, steeped in age-old class divisions, not actual, quantifiable elements that inherently show that some forms of art are better than others:

> The ideological sleight of hand is subtle and powerful: the dominant group's cultural tastes, such as classical music, are institutionalized; institutionalized culture is then interpreted as "high culture," it is presented as proof of their cultural, and by implication, social superiority; hegemonic culture is sacralized. In this way, culture becomes a means of establishing and reinforcing social difference. It is a "weapon in strategies of [social] distinction. It is a way of excluding the Other.[5]

In his analysis, the merit of an artistic piece comes (at least in part) from the value created as we interact with it. This brings to mind the work surrounding affective space and the Magisteria-Ibiza Spectrum[6] that Marsh and Roberts introduced in their work, *Personal Jesus*. In a nutshell, the concept of affective space centers on what's actually happening when an individual encounters and interacts with art.[7] It is understood that there are mental and emotional engagements happening in these moments. I believe we can even make the case for affective space to include physical and spiritual facets. Noise Rock provides a new way for faith to be embodied and to be experienced.

4. Farrell, *Collaborative Circles*, 7.
5. Partridge, *Lyre of Orpheus*, 26.
6. Marsh and Roberts, *Personal Jesus*, 17.
7. Marsh and Roberts, *Personal Jesus*, 16–17.

I return to the chorus of my Preface: there are few moments as potent as throwing yourself at another human being, colliding in violence, joy, passion, and frenetic energy. In the pit, all become equal. In the thundering bass lines, the pummeling drumming and interweaving guitar riffs, there are moments where I have seen beyond myself, where my place in humanity and the universe becomes crystal clear. I am humbled, emboldened, overcome, and transfixed, as music rises, crests, and crashes, wave after wave hitting me in an almost tangible fashion. I have lived through a few key moments of transcendence in my life . . . and several of them have taken place at metal, punk, hardcore, and noise shows.

Returning to Partridge, he makes the case that, while we can continue to judge the merits of certain art within the boundaries of its own form, it's almost impossible (or at least, ill-advised) to try to compare works that traditionally fall along the high/low (or pop) art divides.[8] We might compare classical composers with other classical composers, for instance, but it's a fool's errand to try to pit the merits of Rachmaninoff vs. Rage Against the Machine. As we established earlier, certain genres and forms of folk/low music have certainly been vilified over the years.[9] But what if we shifted our approach and it was not a matter of full rejection or blanket acceptance, but more of an open dialogue with the music itself and its makers and participants? Partridge believes that music has the ability to work on the liminal edge, skirting some of the barriers of logical thought by striking straight at the heart and gut, and thus potentially shaping behavior and belief. To give credit where credit is due, this is an aspect of heavy music that critics are correct to bring up. Music has an inherent power to alter moods, inspire, enrage, entice, and otherwise deeply impact someone's life. These same critics tend to go amiss, however, in a two-fold fashion:

1. They focus on these genres to the exclusion of others that can be equally persuasive and/or damaging.
2. In talking about the power of heavy music to impact people's lives, they don't acknowledge that this can also work in a myriad of positive ways.

There are certain virtues (for lack of a better term) that are always true: compassion, love, mercy, provisions for the day, and so on. Noise Rock has the ability to speak directly into these areas due to its very willingness to

---

8. Partridge, *Lyre of Orpheus*, 26–27.
9. Partridge, *Lyre of Orpheus*, 64.

transgress social norms, to question the social constructs that have been agreed upon by the majority in power. Ken Stephenson surmises that even the structure of modern music (the way the songs are composed) makes room for uncertainty and questioning faith in traditional centers of power.[10] The Chariot (a band that brilliantly melded noise with hardcore punk) makes this questioning explicit in their song "Cheek," both through the song structure and the vocals. Rather than a traditional verse-chorus-verse-chorus-bridge-chorus organization, the track is primarily built on a single, relatively simple guitar riff. In a more conventional composition, it would be an intro guitar line, meant to be heard for a few bars and then the song would move on. Instead, it last for nearly 4:30 of the tracks overall running time of 5:49. During this timeframe, the vocals consist of a mix of lead singer Josh Scogin screaming an initial verse, only to be overtaken by Charlie Chaplin's famous monologue from *The General*. This excerpt calls world powers to task for dehumanizing humanity, making them slaves and pawns in ongoing power struggles. Once this is delivered, Scogin returns for his final vocal assault, while the music rages and burns, finally letting loose after being confined to the opening guitar riff for so long.[11]

Michael Iafrate takes this a step further, and in so doing, makes it even more explicitly theological, by connecting this behavior directly back into the very ethos of what makes Punk Rock, Punk Rock:

> First, "staying punk" as a theologian will require my theological production to be committed rather than neutral or objective. Practitioners of punk theologies will admit . . . that "the punks are right: the world is fucked up, and we need to do something about it," and we will align ourselves with the various strands of liberation theology, which have challenged theologians to commit to the struggle for justice as the first step in the work that they do.[12]

In so doing, Iafrate argues that we can also pursue an approach to faith and theology that is ultimately more egalitarian and more open. By pushing against the gatekeepers of power in all areas of life, a "punk" theology enables all people to have a voice:

> If anything, a punk take on theology must insist that everyone has a theological voice, not only theological experts or magisterial defenders of ecclesial traditions, and that the voices of those on the

---

10. Stephenson, *What to Listen for in Rock*, 26–27.
11. Chariot, "Cheek."
12. Iafrate, "More Than Music," 51.

margins, those often deemed "indecent," are voices to which we must attend and to which we must indeed amplify. This commitment challenges not only ecclesial leaders who imagine themselves as the only spokespersons for their traditions, but also theologians who still tend to not take the voices of average people seriously.[13]

Trevor Hart taps into some of these themes as well, as he brilliantly reminds us that art itself is a "stolen good" and that participation and creation of any sort amounts to rebellion. Noise rock is nothing if not rebellious:

> In our enjoyment of art, therefore, we are technically receivers of stolen goods passed on to us by the various "fences" who paint, write, compose, sculpt or whatever. Indeed, since only the gods can truly create at all, acts of human poesis result at best in a series of clever fakes or imitations of the genuine article. . . . Art, on such an accounting, is inherently transgressive of the limits which creation sets, and thereby constitutes an offence to the divine creativity which it emulates. The aspiration to participate in some sense in a creativity akin to God's original creative act is, in other words, inherently rebellious.[14]

Lastly, Noise Rock (and other forms of heavy music), through its embrace of pain, brokenness, hurting and the need for cathartic shared experiences, provides a fuller space for lament. This is something that is deeply lacking in many music genres today and, perhaps most glaringly, is absent within the church itself. Our current songs of praise and worship scarcely acknowledge the deep wounds that many (all?) of us carry on a daily basis. We need outlets for lament, both for our own health and the health of our relationships with others who are suffering. Indeed, in this particular moment of misinformation, conspiracy theories, disinformation, and general uncertainty with who and what we can trust, we need truth from wherever it might arise. As Johnston reflects,

> When those of other faith traditions live out "Gospel values," thinks D'Costa, the Spirit may be at work in and through them, as John Paul II recognized. Rather than prejudge such thought and action as godless, it is better to have a hermeneutic of open generosity and possibility.[15]

---

13. Iafrate, "More Than Music," 53.
14. Hart, "Through the Arts," 6.
15. Johnston, *God's Wider Presence*, 214.

Thrice's "Death From Above" achieves this identification with the suffering of others by putting the listener inside the thought processes of a military drone operator, questioning everything that he/she does for a living: "But I am never sure who I am killing. How many innocents were in the building? I drop death out of the . . . No longer human beings, no longer people. Just targets on a screen, none of it's real. I drop death out of the sky. . . . Tell me why"[16] If we put a strong face on and simply sing/perform uplifting songs ad nauseam, we risk alienating those who are truly hurting and thus pushing them away from the Spirit who can heal and bind up those wounds. We make ourselves into a community of followers who are only capable of dog-paddling in the shallows, rather than swimmers who can plunge into the abyss with those who are drowning in sorrows.

> What popular music actually achieves—at its best, when taken seriously by its fans—should invite us to reflect on the potential dangers of treating sacramental theology and practice too narrowly. It is too easy to allow the two or seven sacraments used within our own traditions to prevent our seeing how God acts in many ways outside of church practices. . . . When Christians have a negative view of "the world," they may miss the action of God's incarnate Spirit in the world. . . . If Christians are not open to God's action beyond church life, then their faith is impoverished.[17]

We are more fully present, more fully embodied when we allow ourselves to be open to the entire world, not just what is "safe" within Christian subculture, or indeed, within the walls of our churches.

Liberation

Ultimately, if we believe that God moves in and through all things and that Jesus was sent to redeem all of creation (thank you, Athanasius), then there are no genres or expressions of music that exist outside or beyond his love and creative care. As just referenced, this is an extension of Johnston's hermeneutic of open generosity and possibility. Weaving in the previous thoughts about descriptive vs. prescriptive approaches to artistic expressions, I believe that we need to be looking for theological frameworks that broaden our horizons for engagement with the cultural traces of Noise Rock, rather than ones that risk shutting off avenues of discussion.

16. Thrice, "Death From Above."
17. Marsh and Roberts, *Personal Jesus*, 179.

To that end, I believe that one of the most life-giving interpretive models is the one that we find in the field of black liberation theology. At the risk of pitting sacramental theology against liberation theology, Clive Marsh talks about how sacramental theology doesn't always make room for expressions that fall outside of direct revelation/understanding of God and God's grace:

> In Christian understanding, a sacramental theology provides a basis for any aspect of popular culture's becoming a channel of the self-revelation of God, or of the grace of God. This therefore is a theology for such an approach. It does not yet tell us anything about what a theology might be that results from engagement with popular music.[18]

Marsh cites Charles Taylor's assertion that Western (and I might go further to suggest that it's largely a Protestant issue) hang-ups about our bodies have led us to avoid any models that might otherwise force us to acknowledge and reckon with our bodies and the physical space that they take up and the needs that they require.

> Charles Taylor contends that unresolved issues around bodily desire remain at the heart of Western culture. This results in the periodic sidelining of the body within Christianity and across society in general. In the context of Christianity, he calls this process "'excarnation,' the steady disembodying of spiritual life, so that it is less and less carried in deeply meaningful bodily forms, and lies more and more in the head."[19]

It's a tact that has led many Christian communities to have an impoverished, disconnected understanding of suffering. What if art (and theology) that allows no space for suffering and the expression of lament is in fact detrimental to the work and presence of the Spirit? If the Spirit is our comforter, there is no room for solace in purely victorious, triumphalist art. Where there is no lack, no pain, there is no need for comfort. What if our pneumatology has been weakened to the point that certain forms of music are actively keeping out the member of the Trinity whose presence is available to us at any time day or night? A theology that understands pain and suffering, much like the various strains of liberation theology, is one that has room carved out for the Spirit.

---

18. Marsh and Roberts, *Personal Jesus*, 37.
19. Marsh and Roberts, *Personal Jesus*, 38.

What if we approached our understanding of Noise Rock in a similar fashion? That which is fully embodied and authentic about the representation of pain and suffering is that which makes the most space for the presence and movement of the Spirit. The embodied theological method of black liberation theology as demonstrated by Cone's reliance on the black experience in America provides us with another possible model for understanding a better integration of faith and Noise (Rock). Cone's work in liberation theology is a veritable dunking into the deep end of a cold pool for anyone who grew up in a largely disembodied tradition, like myself in the Calvinist reformed Presbyterian churches of my youth. Faith and belief was a matter of doctrinal rectitude, figuring out exactly what Scripture has to say about any given topic and then holding fast to that conviction. You had to get your head right about God and then everything would follow. But Cone's landmark work in the field of liberation theology turns all of that on its head. What good is one's theology if it is not fully embodied? And what good is it if it forces others to be less fully embodied? What if whiteness aligned with a disembodied theology in America has led to the subjugation of others and, as a result, is a theology of evil and destruction instead of life and grace?[20] What if this is true mostly in white Christianity, due to centuries of controlling and overseeing the bodies of others? The curse of owning and dismembering the bodies of others is that we ourselves become more and more disconnected from our own in order to make peace with an existence that claims to love God but enslaves his children. This is where the brilliance of bands like Oxbow and God Bullies comes into play: by pushing back on those systems and remembering what it is like to be fully human, they both rebel against what our predominant culture has told us is "normal," both musically and humanly-speaking.

Indeed, this is something that Sorett illustrates brilliantly in *Spirit in the Dark*, which we explored briefly in dialogue with Oxbow, and to which I want to return more fully now. Named after an Aretha Franklin album, this text explores the tradition of black faith and black art in America. Sorett builds a compelling case that, in part due to slavery and persecution, black Americans never completely bifurcated their religious and artistic experiences and expressions.[21] The jukebox joints and the Sunday morning

---

20. Cone, *Black Theology of Liberation*, 4.

21. "From the 1920s through the 1960s, the coupling of church and spirit provided a language for interpreting and negotiating the complicated cultural and social landscapes that resulted from the events transforming black life, whether those were the mass migrations of the first half of the twentieth century or the civil rights and Black Power

services bled into each other by way of their musicians and singers simply because that's the way they lived their lives. While he suggests that there was some wrestling within various black communities about whether or not they should be singing in night clubs and church services all in the same week, the basic approach was one of integration. And why wouldn't it be? Why divide oneself against oneself? Especially when the outside white culture was already trying to do that and had been doing it for centuries?

The portrait that Sorett paints is a compelling one that allows for a broad range of expressions, both within music by way of genre definitions and within the faith traditions of various black communities in America. He tracks the development of black music throughout the early-to-mid twentieth century and demonstrates how, time and again, the living out of one's faith and the expression of one's art in black culture were not mutually exclusive. You could believe and wrestle with the "ultimate" questions and still live an integrated and human life, fully engaged in the elements of existence that make us finite, fallible creatures.

Now this might not seem all that revolutionary on the surface of it. It's entirely possible that some white Christians are so used to seeing black singers and musicians move effortlessly between the varying worlds of music, like Aretha or Marvin Gaye or Stevie Wonder, that what Sorett is describing might not be all that shocking or compelling. But I would humbly submit, based on my own experiences growing up in the South, in predominantly white churches and completely surrounded by the Contemporary Christian subculture (again, a largely white construct), what Sorett outlines has potential for effecting a paradigm shift for the white evangelical experience in the United States.

So much energy and handwringing of my childhood and early teen years was spent being deeply concerned about whether such-and-such an artist was a Christian musician or not.[22] Are they sacred or secular? Are

---

movements that followed.... During these decades, religion provided crucial source material for constructing norms for a racial art and culture.... Ultimately, appeals to church and spirit offered a rubric pliable and expansive enough for artists and intellectuals, and religious leaders and laypersons, to both affirm and disavow a wide range of religious ideas and practices" (Sorett, *Spirit in the Dark*, 9).

22. Anecdotally, I grew up in a period of the Contemporary Christian Music subculture where the greatest potential area of stumbling and backsliding for a Christian artist had to do with whether or not they had "crossed over" into the secular market. This plagued solo artists like Amy Grant and Michael W. Smith, and groups like dc Talk and Switchfoot. Getting play on a secular radio station or having a music video on MTV was both an opportunity to be heard and seen by whole new audiences... and also risk being

their lyrics clean? What does their lifestyle promote? How often do they talk about God? It's a false dichotomy that leads to madness. It's splitting an atom that was never meant to be halved. The presence of the Spirit can move and fill any space. To live as if it were otherwise (and limited by the power of human will, no less) is to live spiritually bound and gagged. Once again, think back to the bands we've explored thus far: Butthole Surfers, God Bullies, Oxbow, The Jesus Lizard ... even Barkmarket and Cows from the introduction. All of these bands obliterate the sacred/secular, sacred/profane structures. They offer up a path forward in a manner that sets those rules aside so that we can once again explore what it is to be more fully human and more at home in our own skin.

In his book, *The Spirituals and the Blues*, Dr. Cone argues that the blues exist as a musical expression of what it means to be black in America, saying, "I am therefore convinced that it is not possible to render an authentic interpretation of black music without having shared and participated in the experience that created it. Black music must be *lived* before it can be understood."[23] Elsewhere, Cone suggests that black music is "an artistic rebellion against the humiliating deadness of western culture. Black music is political because in its rejection of white cultural values, it affirms the political 'otherness' of black people."[24] I want to tread carefully here, both in the desire to avoid any semblance of cultural appropriation and to avoid smoothing over the incredibly weird and jagged landscape that is Noise Rock. But if I can riff on Cone for just a moment, I think that, taking cues from black liberation theology, we can build a theological framework of engagement with Noise Rock wherein it can be partially interpreted as a lived, embodied expression from within predominately white, male spaces.

On a side note, I am deeply grateful that Noise Rock is not confined solely to white American men. While I have kept the exploration of specific bands here narrow out of necessity, there are many bands in the genre that include a greater spectrum of voices and perspectives, among them: Lydia Lunch, Le Butcherettes, Melt-Banana, Pussy Galore, Boss Hog, Babes in Toyland, Distorted Pony, Royal Trux, Mount Shasta ... and

---

stamped the black sheep of the CCM world and thus wider evangelical Christian culture. My exposure to this line of thinking got even deeper in the years that I worked for the Billy Graham Evangelistic Association, where entire video projects risked being scuttled because Jeremy Camp was wearing his earrings on camera, or the arm of one of the members of Mercy Me had to be cropped out of a photo due to his tattoos being visible.

23. Cone, *Spirituals and the Blues*, 5.
24. Cone, *Spirituals and the Blues*, 6.

this is far from an exhaustive list. Additionally, there are bands/scenes of Noise Rock around the world, especially in Japan, England, France, and Finland. All of these are focal points of research and writing that I hope to pursue in the future.

With all that said, at its best, Noise Rock exists explicitly to dismantle those aforementioned spaces, taking a sonic sledgehammer to men and systems of power, tearing them down from the inside out. And it does precisely that by tapping into weakness.

Weakness

One of the great idols of the American Church is power. It's what helped usher Trump into power (the backing of a largely white Evangelical base). It leads us to cheer when famous bands or celebrities "find God." So much ink has been spilled over the past few decades marveling at the beliefs of U2 and now the same fervor is being lent to Kanye West and his conversion to a form of the faith that the American Church deems as acceptable. The idea of "making Jesus famous" fills our pulpits and floats on the lyrics of the worship songs we sing. It's the twenty-first-century version of "standing up for Jesus" and declaring one's faith in the public square.[25] It's one of the primary elements that facilitated the rise of the televangelists of the 1970s and 1980s, and that drives the engine of the megachurches of the 2000s to now.

The logic of the passion behind this idea seems to be like this: If we make Jesus famous, or if someone famous starts following Jesus, then everyone will know about him and it'll help spread the Gospel. Eventually enough people will hear about him and get saved and then our number one job of the Great Commission will be complete and he'll be able to return and then we'll get whisked away from here and paradise will begin. The appeal is certainly understandable. Isn't that what we all should want? For everyone to be saved and for Jesus to be king? That every knee should bow and every tongue confess? We just need fame and power to make it happen. It only seems logical.

And yet, something is off. Power isn't what Jesus went for when he was here among us. In fact, we're told via Paul that Jesus specifically emptied

---

25. George Duffield's 1858 hymn "Stand Up, Stand Up For Jesus" comes to mind: "Stand up, stand up for Jesus, ye soldiers of the cross; lift high his royal banner, it must not suffer loss. From vict'ry unto vict'ry, his army he shall lead, till ev'ry foe is vanquished and Christ is Lord indeed."

himself of his power and let go of it. Story after story about him shows someone who is deeply concerned for the cast-offs and the forgotten of the world. The light that Jesus brought to this world was often spent illuminating and humanizing those who'd had their humanity removed by disease, social structure, economic need, gender, and more. And this is where John D. Caputo's work fleshing out a theology of weakness (or a theology of the unconditional, to use his terminology) offers a ray of hope for those of us frustrated and worn thin by a theology of power and fame: "The unconditional is not a winning strategy and theology is not about winning."[26]

Caputo suggests, rather than constantly veering towards the sovereignty and rule of God, that we would be better served if we embraced an understanding of the divine that rested in the risks and weakness of the cross. When Scripture talks about the folly of God in comparison with the wisdom of humankind, Caputo says that we would do well to push further into that folly, into the absurdity of a plan that would include salvation through death. Not just death, but the type of death that crucifixion was in that day and age, with all its social implications and horrific forms of suffering. This is a plan that doesn't make sense in any framework other than a theology of weakness.

Remember my earlier description of Noise Rock as the court jester of the music world? It's a genre that risks a certain level of derision and mockery for the sake of highlighting the foibles and pitfalls of our existence. Caputo feels similarly about a theology of the unconditional:

> My claim is that a theology of the unconditional is where a theology of the cross leads; it is the way to follow the way of the cross. When we run into the heroes of the unconditional, the right religious and theological reaction is, What folly! Quelle folie! How mad! The line between a fool and a hero has always been notoriously thin. The wager behind a theology of the unconditional is that there is another strength and wisdom lodged within weakness and folly, one that the street smart world will treat with scorn.[27]

And even further still:

> I propose a fool's logic, theologia as morologia, the foolish nonsense (moria) of the unconditional. A crucified God and crucified theology, both left humbled, hanging naked and deprived of glory—but, once again, all this is in service not of simple death

26. Caputo, *Folly of God*, 5.
27. Caputo, *Folly of God*, 5.

and destruction but of life, just as resurrection follows crucifixion. That is our challenge.[28]

So what would this theology look like for us in lay terms? For Caputo, much of it rests in that idea of emptying. He sees Jesus' act of emptying himself of his power as a pivotal moment where the unconditional (the undeconstructible aspects of God, that which we can't fully reduce or comprehend) calls to all of creation. The work of God in the world is dependent, at least in part, on whether we respond to the quiet invitation, the voice in the middle of the night that welcomes (yet doesn't force) us to action. It's what brings Caputo to this compelling, confounding, and thought-provoking idea: God doesn't exist, but insists.[29] Power is existence, making oneself widely known, whether people are ready for it or not. Weakness is insistence, invitation to something more, when you're ready to take ownership and live into the vision for a kingdom that upends the power dynamics of the world. It is an upending of expectations, much as the narrator of Ecclesiastes does when they say, "All is vanity and a chasing after wind" (Eccl 1:14, NRSV). This portion of the text is so well-known, as the narrator lays out their accomplishments, all they have seen, done, conquered, experienced . . . all the wisdom that's been gained. And it leads to nothingness. The sound of the rushing wind.

And so, to this end, I would like to suggest (to insist) that our obsession with power and influence in art (and specifically music) is leading us to cause parallel tracks of damage that occur when we idolize power in other areas of life. For every U2, there are hundreds of other bands who are already at work on the fringes, wrestling deeply with profound questions of faith, divinity, and the issues that are at the core of what it means to be human in a world full of brokenness and pain. These bands are made up of musicians and vocalists who might not line up with the prevailing cultural wisdom of what is "good" or "catchy" or "popular." Hearkening back to Partridge's thoughts on high vs. low art, these are bands that are likely in the low art category, but as we've seen before, that denomination isn't

---

28. Caputo, *Folly of God*, 5.

29. "The best thing to say is that the unconditional does not exist; it insists. The folly of the unconditional is not to exist. The unconditional calls, lures, solicits, provokes, spooks, and haunts—but it does not have the good sense to exist, so do not rush to the conclusion that there is a reassuring entity up there or down here which does the calling, luring, spooking, etc. . . . The folly of God is that God does not exist. God insists, but God does not exist. . . . The unconditional is a homeless, uncanny sort of thing or no-thing that does not inhabit the house of being" (Caputo, *Folly of God*, 78).

worth much. But these are bands that exist in a more embodied manner in their communities and regions, with performances that are more accessible for those without the financial means or freedom of time to attend the mass events that world famous artists often demand. Their shows cost five or ten dollars, their merch is affordable, they host meals before their performances to hang out with supporters in the towns where they tour. While this isn't the exclusive purview of Noise Rock, and indeed, a few bands within the genre have risen to a level of greater fame and acclaim, this sort of lower level existence is the bread and butter of this scene. Most of the groups mentioned throughout these chapters have fervent and vocal fanbases, yet they are almost all working class bands.

This isn't to say that name-brand bands are somehow bad or evil, but our obsession with power, celebrity, and significance might indeed be somewhat harmful to our psyches. If the end goal of creating music is a worldwide platform, we might need to do some serious introspection into why that's the case. From a purely financial standpoint, bands of that magnitude don't need us. They've crossed over from being an artistic endeavor into one that is geared towards the creating and sustaining of capital. And might I suggest that we don't need bands on that level for our own well-being. We need groups that we can interact with locally, outsiders that know us and that we can know, creating art that speaks to our situations, and into the details that massive bands could never know.

If we have musicians and bands creating art that examines what's going on within and without us in our deepest places, then it will be, by default, spiritual, as we are spiritual beings at our cores. As John Caputo might say, the music cannot be secular, because the music is already theological:

> A theology of culture does not mean applying theology as a prior and independent enterprise to culture, but that theology is a theology of culture, an analysis of the depth dimension in culture, of what is deepest about culture, our cultural lives, our beliefs and practices, ourselves. The culture then is not secular but always already theological.[30]

Additionally, our addiction to power risks blinding us to what else might be possible, both musically and theologically. Inasmuch as Noise Rock continues to push musical boundaries, sonic limits, and so on, Caputo's

---

30. Caputo, *Folly of God*, 40.

approach to theology pushes us to the madness of what it is that we say we actually believe.[31]

> Something deeper is urging us to think beyond the limits of what we have thought and imagined so far. Something is pushing us past the limits, telling us to go where we cannot go, to do what cannot be done, to desire with a desire beyond desire—and so forth. This very expression "and so forth" means that the process just goes on and on, but always deeper and deeper, not higher and higher![32]

By often eschewing traditional song structures, catchy vocals, ear-pleasing production and sound mixing, Noise Rock invites (and challenges) the listener to dive further into the sounds and noises of the genre. While on the face of things it must surely feel like an all-out assault on the ears and brain, patient and attentive listening reveals layers and a certain sense of purpose that goes beyond the surface levels of casual engagement with music.

Embodiment

In sum, we live in a time where so much is conspiring to separate us from ourselves. We need regular reminders to be present in our own bodies. We need help unlearning the hatred with which so many marketing messages train us to view our own frames. Transgression helps us push against and break through boundaries that don't need to exist. Liberation reminds us that finding genuine freedom often comes through trusting our own lived experiences and allowing them to inform our faith. Lastly, Weakness is the much needed antidote to a culture that idolizes power in so many of its forms. These three threads of theology provide vital frameworks for growing us in that direction, giving us permission (as if it were truly needed) to be more fully embodied. Jesus' life itself was that permission, but we lose sight of that far too often. It might feel silly or juvenile to connect Noise Rock to this work, but I think that's exactly what this genre is offering to us, in all its scandalous ways. Dyrness recommends the strength and influence of art (music included) as something that is deeply important for believers:

---

31. "If the cardinal virtues are the virtues of a sane and measured life, the theological virtues are slightly mad, pure folly, practicing the virtues of the spooked—of those who are haunted by the unforeseeable, the undeconstructible, the unconditional, the impossible" (Caputo, *Folly of God*, 36).

32. Caputo, *Folly of God*, 21.

Unlike "signs," which point to reality, symbols participate in the power of what they represent. As Tillich put it, "They open up dimensions of reality which cannot be grasped any other way." Art, then, is important to religion, but more particularly to the person of faith. Art that becomes symbolic of the ground of being can help people understand that they are grasped by the power of being, in a way parallel to the way that symbolic statements like "Christ is the Savior" function for believers.[33]

We desperately need art to remind us of who we are, in all our frailties and our strengths.

From an audience reception standpoint, we can also see embodiment being worked out in the various ways that listeners participate with the bands within the genre. This examination itself could be its own book or series of podcast discussions, a new extension of *The Decline of Western Civilization* focused specifically on noise rock, if you will. But as a quick overview, these steps of engagement include listening, attending shows, buying artifacts of the music itself (records, CDs, tapes, USB drives with music files preloaded, etc.), collecting merchandise, starting 'zines, creating labels to more formally support and put out the music from these bands, and in our online age of digital living, creating Facebook groups, Discord communities, and updating databases like Discogs and Wikipedia to more accurately reflect the story and life of a band. In this regard, the lineage from punk to noise rock is clear: rather than having a barrier between audience and artists, these lines blur constantly, especially in live performances where band members sometimes leave the stage (if indeed there even is a stage) to interact with the crowd, or when eager fans rush the stage to thrash alongside the band or to yell into the mic and then launch themselves back into the audience to crowd surf. That blurring extends into those other communal areas mentioned above. Before the internet existed, zines often functioned as a sort of music network, bringing together like-minded individuals, sharing news and interviews about bands as they would tour across regions of the country.

One of the most notable examples of this is one we encountered briefly earlier, Touch and Go, currently based out of Chicago. Touch and Go started as a zine in 1979, founded by Tesco Vee and Dave Stimson in Lansing, MI. At the beginning, the focus of the zine was on punk and hardcore music, but noise rock was quickly brought into the fold as well,

---

33. Dyrness, *Poetic Theology*, 113.

when Vee (who was also the frontman for the punk band, The Meatmen) brought on Corey Rusk in the early 1980s to help run Touch and Go Records, the music label that grew out as a natural extension of the zine. Rusk was himself a musician as well, playing bass in the band Necros. This blending of the roles, the overlap of musicians as writers, musicians as documenters of the scenes in which they were a part, is a potent aspect of the DIY nature of these genres. In one of the introductions for *Touch and Go: The Complete Hardcore Punk Zine '79–'83*, Vee reflected on the motivations that led to its creation:

> Oh the indelible mark the illustrious fanzine (root word: fan) hath left on cultural movements/musical happenstances o'er the last six decades. The unofficial and unprofessional aspect of the homemade zine is what drew Masters Dave Stimson and Bob Vermeulen into the enterprise known as *Touch and Go* magazine three decades ago. Crafting a fanzine was certainly nothing new, but in mid-Michigan we were breaking ground, breaking wind, and generally feeling our way thru the process, with nothing to guide us but disdain for what was and a need for the new, whether "the new" meant Black Flag, The Feelies, The Specials, or Throbbing Gristle.[34]

His cofounder (and coauthor) Dave Stimson continued that trajectory and thought process, saying,

> We were simply living in the moment; that's what you do when you're young and think you know it all.... Now, and I can't stress this enough, *T&G* never would have happened if we (the Vee man and me) didn't have that shared, near-maniacal passion for the exact same music, and I mean the exact same music.[35]

This passion that both Vee and Stimson share is crucial for a fuller embodiment with these genres of music. Once Touch and Go Records launched, it quickly became a home for notable noise rock bands like Butthole Surfers, Big Black, Killdozer, Scratch Acid, The Jesus Lizard, and Shellac (among many others). As Rusk noted, through the zine and the efforts of Vee and Stimson,

> this stream of creativity and productivity on their part was contributing to a Michigan-area scene that was starting to have some

---

34. Vee and Stimson, *Touch and Go*, x.
35. Vee and Stimson, *Touch and Go*, xiv.

notable bands of its own. By 1981, Tesco and Dave were not satisfied to merely document the music around them on paper alone, so '81 saw the release of the first records on the brand new Touch and Go Records label. Necros, the Fix, and a compilation that included a cut by Tesco's own band, the Meatmen, put Michigan and Ohio on the punk rock vinyl map.[36]

The creativity can't be contained and spills out in all directions. The audience eats the music and becomes musicians themselves. The local area responds to these incarnations and in turn births new art. Touch and Go is just one example of how this can take place, morphing from the written word celebrating music into purveyors of new music that captures that same imagination and drive that first led to documenting it. This is not to say that every single noise rock band in existence has spawned this level of passion and commitment, but there is something vital that has happened and continues to happen in these spaces because, as a genre, it can be a conduit, drawing upon broken sounds, disjointed rhythms, and scattershot vocals to form new auditory expressions of embodiment.

36. Vee and Stimson, *Touch and Go*, xxii–xxiii.

Chapter 7
A Theology of Noise/Rock

PLAYLIST:

"give/UP"—Le Butcherettes

"Tainted In Sin"—Le Butcherettes

"Demon Stuck In Your Eye"—Le Butcherettes

"Drugs On The Bus"—Crystal Fairy

"Rebel Girl"—Melvins feat. Teri Gender Bender

"Brood of Vipers"—QOHELETH

"Uterine"—QOHELETH

"The Clearing at The End is The Path"—QOHELETH

Scan for Playlist

We arrive then, finally, at our destination, albeit a temporary one, as there remains so much more work, research, listening, and storytelling to be done. The threads of chaos, ambiguity, embodiment, transgression, noise, music, sound, liberation, weakness . . . they all lead here. What does a theology of Noise/Rock sound like? How might it function in our lives? And where can it lead us in our exploration and understand of the Divine? How might we hear the *Sonus Dei* in our everyday existence? Why does this matter theologically? And why does it matter now, of all times? I believe a theology of Noise/Rock can be built upon four key elements:

1. More attentive/active listening ears.
2. More receptive/empathetic hearts towards others.
3. Attuned minds/souls for navigating the chaos of our current era.
4. Developing new tongues/languages.

Taken in sum, these four elements offer us a path towards a more loving, grace-filled, fully embodied and generous approach to both ourselves and perhaps even God, Son, and Spirit. At the heart of these four elements is one central assertion: whenever God shows up in the various books of Scripture, God is usually accompanied by noise and/or sound of some sort. Obviously, it is impossible to know exactly what sounds the authors of the these texts had in mind, so using our imagination in general will be necessary for developing an understanding for the *Sonus Dei*. But we don't have to go far to get a sense of just how "noisy" God is:

- Speaking creation into existence. (Gen 1:3–31)
- The sounds made in the Garden of Eden that caused Adam and Eve to hide. (Gen 3:8–10)
- God speaking to Hagar and Hagar naming God. (Gen 16)
- Skin scraping skin as Jacob wrestled with God. (Gen 32)
- The crackling of the burning bush, not to mention God's voice itself. (Exod 3)
- Chaotic noises of the ten plagues. (Exod 7–12)
- The rush of air in a pillar of smoke, the sizzling and popping in a pillar of fire. (Exod 13)
- The swirling waters of the Red Sea being parted. (Exod 14)

- Bones rattling and being rejoined together, sinew stretching, skin reforming over muscle and tissue. (Ezek 37:4–9)[1]
- The searing of the air as fire fell from the heavens, igniting Elijah's sacrificial pyre. (1 Kgs 18)
- The thunder overtaking the disciples' boat and Jesus' snores before they woke him. (Matt 8:23–27)
- The crunch and heavy thud as the stone rolled away from the entrance of the tomb. (Matt 28:1–8)
- Fish splashing and jumping as overflowing nets are dragged into the boats. (Luke 5:1–10)
- Jesus drawing in the sand with his finger. (John 8:1–11)
- Sobbing sounds as Jesus wept over Lazarus's death. (John 11)
- Gentle rustling as Thomas brushes Jesus' skin, witnessing his wounds. (John 20:20–29)

God is present to us in these and many more sounds throughout the texts. I can't shake the core thought that maybe, just maybe, many of the noises we encounter in our lives are echoes and reverberations of the initial sound waves that rippled across the deep, breathing new life, light, water, land . . . everything. *Sonus Dei* is embedded into creation itself, including us. Which means that perhaps God can be more present to us now, the more carefully we listen, the more accustomed our ears can become to noises and sounds, voices and chaos that we typically shut out.

Active Ears

At the risk of being overly simplistic, this journey into a theology of noise/rock has to begin with our ears. How are we using them? How carefully are

---

1. "Then he said to me, 'Prophesy to these bones, and say to them: O dry bones, hear the word of the Lord. Thus says the Lord God to these bones: I will cause breath to enter you, and you shall live. I will lay sinews on you, and will cause flesh to come upon you, and cover you with skin, and put breath in you, and you shall live; and you shall know that I am the Lord.' So I prophesied as I had been commanded; and as I prophesied, suddenly there was a noise, a rattling, and the bones came together, bone to its bone. I looked, and there were sinews on them, and flesh had come upon them, and skin had covered them; but there was no breath in them. Then he said to me, 'Prophesy to the breath, prophesy, mortal, and say to the breath: Thus says the Lord God: Come from the four winds, O breath, and breathe upon these slain, that they may live'" (Ezek 37:4–9, NRSV).

we listening? Leaning into three specific passages from Exodus, Deuteronomy, and 1 Kings, we can see (hear?) that God's presence itself is nuanced and not binary. God makes God's presence known in multiple ways:

> When all the people witnessed the thunder and lightning, the sound of the trumpet, and the mountain smoking, they were afraid and trembled and stood at a distance. (Exod 20:18, NRSV)

> Then the Lord spoke to you out of the fire. You heard the sound of words but saw no form; there was only a voice. (Deut 4:12, NRSV)

> He said, "Go out and stand on the mountain before the Lord, for the Lord is about to pass by." Now there was a great wind, so strong that it was splitting mountains and breaking rocks in pieces before the Lord, but the Lord was not in the wind; and after the wind an earthquake, but the Lord was not in the earthquake; and after the earthquake a fire, but the Lord was not in the fire; and after the fire a sound of sheer silence. (1 Kgs 19:11–12, NRSV)

God is present in the thunder, the sound of the trumpet, in a voice out of the fire, and yet also not in the wind, not in the earthquake, not in the fire. God is not contained by any one of those elements, yet makes Godself known in the multiplicity of those elements. Whereas God is witnessed in the noise and chaos of Exodus, words seemingly suffice in Deuteronomy. And on the other end of the spectrum, God might not be in those noises, those loud and boisterous moments of 1 Kings, but something about them prepares the way. In this context, the chaos and noise seems to be a sort of ground-clearing. They overwhelm the senses, the ears in a manner that gives way to utter quiet. And in this instance, this silence was where Elijah heard God.

The point being, I don't believe that God communicates with us in one way only. And God's presence isn't only made known to us in one form or fashion. There was a diversity of wavelengths, if you will, in these texts. But getting better at being attuned to multiple wavelengths, sometimes at the same time, requires practice. Our ears need help developing the ability to hear several things at once, isolating key tones, messages wrapped within wavelengths, etc. Learning how to better listen to noise/rock provides us with a form of that practice. Further, learning how noise has been separated and pushed away from other forms of sounds might clue us in as to how we ourselves have separated a more active listening from trying to hear God only when and where we want to. As Hegarty explains, one interpretation of noise is as a negative, that operates as an unwanted presence.[2] It upends what we think we're listening for:

> Noise, and the music that comes from an engagement with it, tests commonplace notions of hearing and listening, and tries to destabilize not just our expectations of content or artistic form, but how we relate to those, to the point where the most interesting point of encounter might be a loss of controlled listening, a failure of adequate hearing, even if this is only temporary.[3]

This is apophatic at its core. Defining God/music by their negatives? Music says who/what God is within certain structures and frameworks, while noise captures some of what God is not, not in the sense that noise is anti-God or opposed to God, but rather in the sense that there are elements and characteristics of God that run counter to everything we think we know, that refuse categorization and refined doctrine, as noise refuses to be boxed in and resists easier demarcations. Try taking out a piece of blank sheet music and notating actual noise, with no sharps, flats, keys, treble or bass clefs. It would be utter madness, much like trying to pin down God and say concretely that God is unequivocally this or that. Returning to Caputo for a moment:

> To think the weakness and folly of God all the way down would consist, accordingly, in resisting the temptation to enter them into an economy of long-term strength and wisdom. . . . What would that be like? It would be like forgiveness, which is folly in the light of the world's wisdom, a weak force whose power lies in the power of abdicating power, abdicating retaliation—no footstools—which we might call the power of powerlessness.[4]

Suppose Caputo's Unconditional is deconstructed music and noise? Hegarty provides us with a compelling link, via, what else? Weakness: "Weakness, in the form of the refusal of dogmatic supremacy or assertion of rules, will remain a central part of noise, and like much that constitutes noise, it arrives through negativity, here from a criticism of a new type of music."[5] Music exists, noise insists. The sheer unknowableness of the

---

2. "Noise is negative: it is unwanted, other not something ordered. It is negatively defined—i.e., by what it is not (not acceptable sound, not music, not valid, not a message or a meaning), but it is also a negativity" (Hegarty, *Noise/Music*, 5).

3. Hegarty, *Noise/Music*, 5.

4. Caputo, *Folly of God*, 61.

5. Hegarty, *Noise/Music*, 48.

Divine is woven throughout noise. Neither can be fully grasped or controlled, identified and quantified fully and completely. The Divine ebbs and flows into and out of our lives, much as tides of noise crash into our shores and then pull back again.

The divide between noise and music even has socio-economic implications, dating back at least to the Industrial Revolution.[6] As life got louder by way of machines and factories and the concentrations of people who worked in them, Hegarty asserts that those with means moved away from the centers of noise in order to obtain peace and quiet,[7] and with them, "high" forms of art.[8] Now it's one thing to suppose that God is found in the quiet, away from the masses of humanity groaning and working away to make a living. It's quite another to hear God's presence elsewhere, in the midst of chaos and upheaval and use that as an invitation to dive deeper into that noise, to reject the framework of high and low art, and with it, the literal separation of some humans from others. Is this not what Jesus did, taking upon himself human form? Humans are nothing if not noisy, and Jesus' physical body brought all that noise with it: crying, sounds of chewing, snoring, farting, moaning, cursing, creaking, popping, laughing, dying. Again, this is not an invitation per se to inundate ourselves with nothing but noise all day long, but rather, it's an opportunity to see where we are no longer listening with attentiveness. Where are we not hearing our neighbors? What wavelengths and signals have we tuned out by way of habit or assumption?

In the same way that we are called to love our neighbors as ourselves, perhaps we are called to love our neighbors' noises as we love our own

---

6. "But with population comes a concentration of wealth, in the proto-capitalist sixteenth to eighteenth centuries. This, combined with a growing concentration of lower classes, brings the phenomenon of street music and performance. Early noise abatement legislation (i.e., from that period) targets street criers and street music. R. Murray Schafer writes that the perception, which heightens in the nineteenth century, is that 'the street had now become the home of non-music, where it mixed with other kinds of sound-swill and sewage'" (Hegarty, *Noise/Music*, 6).

7. "With mechanization, the perception of noise widens and the sounds of industry are associated with the 'noisier' working class, and retain their status as unwanted because low, because not acceptably hierarchized into the forms of 'high' music or meaning" (Hegarty, *Noise/Music*, 6).

8. "Schafer writes that 'with indoor living, two things developed antonymously: the high art of music and noise pollution—for noises were the sounds that were kept outside.' The status of western art music depends on this excluded other, and even doubles this exclusion when it attempts to represent nature or specific sounds within it" (Hegarty, *Noise/Music*, 7).

noises. At the very least, gaining an appreciation for their noises (if not outright love), leads us directly into the second sound element, more gracious and humble hearts.

Empathetic Hearts

What good are hearing ears if the knowledge that comes from listening doesn't lead to some sort of change or transformation? We might as well make ourselves fully deaf if we're not going to allow ourselves to be upended by the humanity of those around us. Again, we can gain some guidance by looking at themes within a few key passages:

> For you have been a refuge to the poor, a refuge to the needy in their distress, a shelter from the rainstorm and a shade from the heat. When the blast of the ruthless was like a winter rainstorm, the noise of aliens like heat in a dry place, you subdued the heat with the shade of clouds; the song of the ruthless was stilled. (Isa 25:4–6, NRSV)

> But the multitude of your foes shall be like small dust, and the multitude of tyrants like flying chaff. And in an instant, suddenly, you will be visited by the Lord of hosts with thunder and earthquake and great noise, with whirlwind and tempest, and the flame of a devouring fire. (Isa 29:5–6, NRSV)

> You have heard that it was said, 'You shall love your neighbor and hate your enemy.' But I say to you, Love your enemies and pray for those who persecute you, so that you may be children of your Father in heaven; for he makes his sun rise on the evil and on the good, and sends rain on the righteous and on the unrighteous. (Matt 5:43–45, NRSV)

The sounds of the rain, the blast of winter storm, the crackling of the heat, the whirlwind, thunder, earthquake . . . once again we find God in the midst of all of these, but this time we find the Other present as well. The list of these includes the poor, the needy, the ruthless, aliens, your neighbor, and your enemy. The passage from Matthew in particular is often referenced as a cornerstone for one of Jesus' most important teachings during his ministry, but sadly, it's not something that we as a country (speaking specifically about the United States) have done well throughout most of our history. Indeed, given the sheer volume of information that we are constantly facing in our daily lives from social media, the 24-hour news cycle, email forwards, texts, etc., it is all too easy to drown out the voices of those around us, even within our own neighborhoods.

But if we are willing to broaden the scope of our listening, via noise/rock, and then further incline our hearts to the voices that we are more capable of hearing, developing a greater sense of empathy to those who are different from us becomes more and more possible. Once again, the very nature of noise itself is perfectly suited to help us upend our own expectations and habits as a means of expanding our understanding of the Other. In exploring and developing an ontology of noise, Hainge touches on the fluid nature of noise and the myriad of ways in which it can be perceived and either rejected or engaged with. He says,

> George Prochnik, tracing a lineage through Nietzsche and Theodor Lessing, suggests that the increase in noise in the modern world is in part the result of the subjugated masses refusing to be silenced, of the oppressed "making a noise" about unjust power relationships'[9]

Even more to our point here about developing an empathy and love for others, he further offers that "noise is imbued with a particular propensity for transgressing and destabilising fixed boundaries."[10]

For better or worse, expanding our personal space and boundaries to accommodate others can sometimes feel like transgression as we're pushed into the unknown (and sometimes the uncomfortable shared regions of having to grow and mature). And yet, noise is also a reminder that

> there is nothing outside of it and because it is in everything. Indeed, noise is not only multi-medial, arising in many different kinds of forms and media, engaging many different senses, sensations, responses and affects, it is medial insofar as it is always in-between, produced in the passing into actuality of everything, both animate and inanimate.[11]

I think noise can provide a reminder that we are far more connected and interdependent on each other than we would some times care to admit. We touched on this in our earlier exploration of what Noise Rock actually is, but there is a totality to noise and the ways in which it is woven into existence itself:

9. Hainge, *Noise Matters*, 9.
10. Hainge, *Noise Matters*, 11.
11. Hainge, *Noise Matters*, 13.

> If noise inhabits everything because everything is in actuality formed out of noise, then what noise ultimately points to is the relational ontology according to which the world comes to pass, the way in which there is nothing that falls outside of the event, of the realm of process, of an existence formed only through the heterogeneous assemblages of different forms of expression which inescapably and incessantly contract the virtual into the actual.[12]

I believe we can extend a version of that totality to humanity itself. In the finite realm, we are all that we have. We can be our own hands and feet of Jesus, so to speak, caring for those in need . . . or we can be the apathetic ones who don't care what happens to our communities, because the problems are *over there*, so to speak and thus they're for someone else to contend with and solve.

---

12. Hainge, *Noise Matters*, 14.

Le Butcherettes, *Don't Bleed* (2020)

Returning to the rock side of the noise rock equation, we're going to spend a little time with a band that comes to us by way of Guadalajara, Mexico. Formed in 2007 by lead singer and guitarist Teresa Suárez Cosío (more commonly known by her stage name "Teri Gender Bender"), Le Butcherettes is a punk/noise rock band that is consistently unafraid of pushing their own musical boundaries, with their latest release, 2020's *DON'T BLEED* bringing in synth/electronic elements that aren't always present in the foundational genres that made up their earlier records. Cosío was born in Denver, Colorado, and later relocated to Mexico after her father died, making her way with her mom and brothers to her mother's homeland.[13] Over the course of the band's existence, they have released five full-length

13. Host, "Le Butcherettes' Teri Gender Bender."

albums, two EPs and multiple singles. Cosío also frequently collaborates with other artists, including Omar Rodríguez-López of At The Drive-In and The Mars Volta fame, Buzz Osborne and Dale Crover of sludge metal legend Melvins, and Red Hot Chili Peppers' guitarist John Frusciante. Two of Rodríguez-López's brothers are long-standing members of Le Butcherettes as well, so these collaborative circles continue to engender a wealth of creative endeavors over the years.

Now up to this juncture, I've made a point of conversing exclusively with US noise rock bands, primarily to keep the focus narrow and to allow for a more in-depth discussion of the particularities of how the US sound developed out of punk and no wave. Le Butcherettes and Cosío provide a compelling bridge to expanding that scope, given her personal history with living in both the States and Mexico, as well as releasing several of their albums on US-based labels. It's an opportunity to listen to and learn from the other, as represented both by the band's collective lived experiences. The Rodríguez-López brothers grew up largely in El Paso, a town literally on the Texas/Mexico border.

Le Butcherettes, *Sin Sin Sin* (2011)

Their perspectives remind me of multiple conversations I've had over the past few years with my friend and mentor Mako Fujimura, as he refers to some artists as "mearcstapas" or border stalkers. In the case of Le Butcherettes, it's both literal and figurative. And as a result, they are a perfect example of what can be offered up via noise rock to help us develop more empathetic hearts by gaining a better understanding of those who are different from us.

In this instance, I am by necessity centering myself, and using those who are different from me to expound on what I need to learn and how I need to grow in my understanding. As a white cis male who grew up in rural South Carolina and within the Protestant tradition, I might be able to conjure up a certain amount of basic human decency level-empathy for the lives and experiences of the members of Le Butcherettes (in a similar fashion that I might be able to so the same for the members of other bands that I've covered thus far). But what makes Teri Gender Bender's voice and music so instructive for me is that she's bringing various perspectives that I simply don't have: female, Mexican descent, and Catholic influences from her upbringing. The art she/they have created over the years presents me (and others) with an invitation (not that it was made *for* us) to dive in and expand the empathetic boundaries of my own heart. What Jesus did naturally as breathing in his walk amongst us is a trait that we have to be diligent to humbly nurture throughout our lives.

And thus, when Cosío talks about her motivation for performing in a blood-stained apron, it's an opportunity to try to truly listen to her experiences and how they manifest in her art and music:

> Exactly, it was symbolism. It was my plea of, "This is how I'm feeling. I feel like I'm a torn-up mess. I feel like a piece of meat." Having to walk to school and walk back having people yell degrading things like, "Mamacita!" All those things sort of building up, and also coming from a very dysfunctional family. So, that inspired me to wear it. What I'm wearing or what I'm doing now comes from a whole different symbolism of honoring my roots, my grandmother. . . . Like, just because I have light skin doesn't mean that it's like, "Oh, there's no way that you're indigenous." There's all this ignorance of what should be what or who should look like what. So, for me, it's being able to be proud of my roots without being ashamed anymore, because when I was living in Denver, there was a lot of shame, especially when my mom would pick me up from school. She didn't really know how to speak English, and the teachers even would make fun of me for that. . . . I'm wearing this to heal myself. I want to be connected to my grandmother. Or when I was wearing the apron with the blood on it, I wanted to just release myself of feeling like a mutilated woman.[14]

Elsewhere, the Catholic influence of guilt on her life and her identities comes fully into view via the 2011 album *Sin Sin Sin*:

> It's also a theme of just feeling. . . . I hate saying I was a victim. I'm not a victim, but just a feeling like a piece of rug fur. That's basically what I think the theme is. That no matter what you do, it feels like you're causing a disturbance to someone, that you're a pest. You're wrong because of the sex that you were born in. *Sin Sin Sin* alludes to the theme of religion. Especially growing up in

14. Silva, "Le Butcherettes."

a Catholic family, you really feel the fear of the devil when you're growing up. That could kind of have a traumatizing effect on you—at least the nightmares, repeated ones—and so it touches those themes, religion, female empowerment and just going forward despite what the white sheep say.[15]

One of the beautiful aspects of developing that more empathetic heart is that, as we navigate the differences and unique perspectives, we are gifted with the realization that commonalities can be found in their midst. While I didn't grow up Catholic, the theme of religious fear that Cosío is reflecting on is something I also know very well, via Protestant doctrines of control that were instilled in me from childhood. As noise rock continues to both mature and mutate, having a multitude of voices within it will only serve to enrich the genre and make it more compelling. My hope is that we take that deepening and diversifying of voices to broaden who we are and who we can be. The *Sonus Dei* is found in the voices of all people.

Attuned Minds

After tackling our ears and our hearts, the third element of a Noise/Rock theology takes shape within our minds. Our thought processes are constantly being invited to take on new forms, theories, concepts, and frameworks. In all honesty, some of it can be exhausting. Depending on how plugged in we are with digital media, the news cycle, and our own social circles, we are inundated daily with information, blasted with the force and pace of a city-full's worth of fire hydrants. Rather than trying to make a case for engaging with all of that data, I want to briefly consider three parables that offer a baseline for how we might engage with perspectives that upend our expectations. From there, we'll look at how a framework like cosmic pessimism might paradoxically bring a sense of hope, and lastly how my own band is attempting to navigate a process of deconstruction, reassessment, creation, and repeat.

In Matthew 20 and Luke 14, we are given three parables from Jesus, each one focused on some sort of societal norm or expectation on how the world is supposed to work. In the first, Jesus compares the kingdom of heaven to a vineyard that needs workers. Various groups of laborers are hired throughout the day, and when it comes time to settle up in the evening, the workers who started earliest are shocked and angered to learn that

15. Host, "Le Butcherettes' Teri Gender Bender."

they are getting paid the same amount as those who started later, even the ones who started closest to the end of the day:

> But he replied to one of them, "Friend, I am doing you no wrong; did you not agree with me for the usual daily wage? Take what belongs to you and go; I choose to give to this last the same as I give to you. Am I not allowed to do what I choose with what belongs to me? Or are you envious because I am generous?" So the last will be first, and the first will be last. (Matt 20:13–16, NRSV)

The landowner (and by extension Jesus himself) doesn't really give a satisfactory answer to why he paid the same amount to everyone, other than to assert his right as the hirer to pay whatever he wants. And it concludes with that in/famous line that truly subverts so many expectations about how the world works, "the last will be first, and the first will be last."

Shifting over to Luke, we are greeted with two similar parables back-to-back, the first running from verses 7–14, and the second from verses 15–24. Both involve celebratory meals and the invited guests to each event. In the first, the subversion comes in the seating arrangement around a wedding banquet table. The listeners are challenged to rethink the practice of grabbing the places of honor, and rather to sit somewhere more humble. Again, there's no guarantee of this happening, but the suggestion is that they might be seen in their humility and raised up by the host (rather than being demoted for selfishly choosing the best seats from the outset). Additionally, the telling of the parable ends with curious admonition:

> When you give a luncheon or a dinner, do not invite your friends or your brothers or your relatives or rich neighbors, in case they may invite you in return, and you would be repaid. But when you give a banquet, invite the poor, the crippled, the lame, and the blind. And you will be blessed, because they cannot repay you, for you will be repaid at the resurrection of the righteous. (Luke 14:7–14, NRSV)

Following immediately on the heels of this, as if to more fully flesh out and illustrate the point, we have the Banquet of Absentee Guests and Empty Seats (my title). Once again, a dinner table is prepared, guests are invited, and yet they all ghost the host, offering a multitude of excuses why they can't make it. In anger, he instructs his servant to:

> "Go out at once into the streets and lanes of the town and bring in the poor, the crippled, the blind, and the lame." And the slave said, "Sir, what you ordered has been done, and there is still

room." Then the master said to the slave, "Go out into the roads and lanes, and compel people to come in, so that my house may be filled. For I tell you, none of those who were invited will taste my dinner." (Luke 14:21–24, NRSV)

At the beginning of this parable, this banquet is likened to the kingdom of God, which makes the interpretation of the ending (including the anger and vindictive nature of the host, presumably the God-figure in the story) even more confusing and strange. But rather than try to explain the contradictions away, I want to lean into the thought that perhaps we need to be diving deeper into contradictions, living in those ambiguous spaces and allowing our minds to get more comfortable with holding ideas in tension and allowing that to in turn free us up from having to cling to dichotomies that ultimately choke the life out of mystery and the unknown.

And speaking of the unknown, as we saw earlier in Thacker's exploration of the landscape of cosmic pessimism in *In The Dust of This Planet*, this is an outlook on life that essentially suggests that humanity doesn't matter to the rest of existence. We looked at his outline of three different sorts of nature that coexist alongside of each other: the world-for-us, the world-in-itself, and the world-without-us. Thacker asserts that there is a little bit of overlap between the first and second and then between the second and third, but virtually none between the first and third. The world-for-us is the plane of existence in which we as humans live: our perspectives are mostly self-centric, we see the world through our own lens as a species and we think that things more or less revolve around us. The world-in-itself is basically the existence of nature, where it often intersects with our world, yet it is distinct and separate from humanity itself. The world-without-us? This is where cosmic pessimism is fully ushered into the discussion. Thacker says that this is the true horror of existence, when we grapple with the thought that the world (the universe, space, time, etc.) doesn't pay any mind to humanity and that it doesn't care whether we live or die. It's the notion that the Milky Way will keep on spinning, regardless of whether or not humanity is thriving on planet Earth or somehow gets completely annihilated. Our lives don't matter one bit to the clockwork of the universe.

While this outlook might seem completely bleak and dark (and make no mistake, it certainly is on one level), if embraced, I would argue that it offers a lot of freedom. If our understanding of existence shifts from one where everything is consequential (only insofar as it concerns us) to one where we are not the center of the universe, we truly have nothing left to fear and a wide opportunity of liberty to create however and whatever we want. Now perhaps this appeals more to someone like me with my anarchist and punk tendencies where I want to embrace the table-flipping, whip-making Jesus driving money-changers out of the temple. But I truly believe that, even if you don't fully subscribe to a world-without-us view of this life, even a partial consideration of it allows so many weights to fall from your shoulders. Maybe everything doesn't have to be life and death? Maybe we can stare into the abyss of unknowing and walk away off-kilter, but not totally insane? And maybe through this, we can start to come to grips with a divine presence that makes no human sense?

Jeffrey F. Keuss, drawing upon the examples of Nick Cave and Tom Waits, explains it in this manner: the artist has the opportunity to help bridge the gulf between knowing and unknowing, keeping the sacred space between uncertainty and certainty open so that others can experience what it is like to encounter God over and over and over again. It is a staring into the face of God, while also somehow maintaining some sort of grasp on the language of humanity so that you can convey to others what you've seen:

> Cave and Waits share this vision whereby God is ultimately acknowledged and embraced in a collapsing of seemingly opposing descriptors—terrible, irrational, incendiary, beautiful—into a singular yet multivalent Holy God that offers an apocalyptic totality and surplus of meaning that only imaginative performativity can begin to see, touch, taste, and hear.[16]
>
> It is the true artist who stands in this troubling gap of meaning that is both found and lost, never to be fixed or locked down but always on the move. Rather than close this fissure by trying to dominate or control meaning by naming God into certitude and therefore away from the active repose of faith, the musician's true vocation is to prevent such closure upon meaning and truth by continually reopening this sacred space through the making of art anew that always points over the next horizon and calls after God again and again and again as if it is the first time and the last time.[17]

David Dault talks about it as "empty communication." It's not that we're saying nothing, it's that what we're saying is empty, pointing at the void and gazing upon the nameless name of Beauty and not knowing how to say anything other than emptiness:

---

16. Keuss, "Tom Waits, Nick Cave, and Martin Heidegger," 164.
17. Keuss, "Tom Waits, Nick Cave, and Martin Heidegger," 165–66.

> As such, the avant-garde gesture offers a third possibility, suspended beyond the apophatic gesture of the negative theologian and the positivity of the scientist. Though it may be misunderstood as an empty refusal to communicate, the avant-garde gesture is instead simply empty communication. Like Grünewald's John the Baptist, the gesture names all the words cannot. It points to the Void, and in pointing, invokes a nameless name for the Beauty of that terrifying frontier. Echoing Reed, it is the pure molten essence of "energy and physicality," confronting the recipient in the vastness of the wave and the vacuousness of the crater, in the blue that is simply blue itself, beyond language but not beyond communication.[18]

Imagine the creative freedom that comes with that perspective!

I love this idea of something beyond both the positive and the apophatic, something that perhaps embraces both, or that sees the contradictions between the two and once again dives straight into the heart of the contradiction. It's very reminiscent of what Michael Novak wrestles with in his book, *The Experience of Nothingness*. Originally written in 1970 (and later revised in 1998) in the wake of the cultural, social, and economic upheaval of the late 1960s (particularly in the shadow of the Vietnam War), it's his attempt at explaining a world coming apart at the seams, with fewer and fewer philosophical underpinnings to satisfactorily help explain what was going on. In confronting moral failings, the inadequacy of current religious frameworks, and continued pain and suffering, the setting led Novak to reflections such as:

> St. John of the Cross, who emphasized the short-circuiting of the human mind under the (so to speak) lightning surge of God. Under excess light, human equipment burns out. For St. John, the encounter with God comes, therefore, as an experience of nothingness: nada y nada y nada.[19]

> For St. John, it meant the emptiness in the soul of those who have sought God, who turned their minds and wills toward Him, and kept them fixed there, in that direction, even though "no one appeared." It is an oddity that those who seek God become quite familiar with the experience of nothingness. . . . Nothingness is

---

18. Dault, "To The Void," 15.
19. Novak, *Experience of Nothingness*, xii–xiii.

familiar terrain to the believer in a transcendent God. It is a terrain traversed in great inner pain.[20]

I would expand that framework even further to allow for those who wouldn't call themselves believers, yet who have done work in their lives to find that transcendent God and have found themselves left wanting. How much disbelief, unbelief, and perhaps even apathy can be chalked up to peering into nothingness and seeing/hearing silence?

QOHELETH, *God Is the Warmest Place to Hide* (2017)

It's in that spirit of contradiction that the band QOHELETH came into existence. This is my group, created with two of my best friends, Mike Strickler and Caiden Withey. Mike and I are the musicians in the band,

---

20. Novak, *Experience of Nothingness*, xiii.

while Caiden is an artist and painter who has shaped our visual presence from the very beginning of our formation. I'm very hesitant to talk about our work in this space, lest it give the impression that I somehow see what we've been creating over the past seven to eight years as existing on the same plane of merit or importance as the other artists and bands that we've explored thus far. While I am deeply proud of what we create, it's hard for me to make any sort of a value judgment about it and prefer to leave those discussions to those with more distance from it. That said, the process of not only researching noise rock but also creating it (or our version of it) consistently for several years in a row has given me some hands-on insights that I might not be able to convey in any other way.

Indeed, because music is capable of short-circuiting what the written word sometimes struggles to communicate, it is tempting to simply say, "Go look up everything we've released, listen to each of our four albums and four EPs on repeat and then you'll know what we've been trying to express." But I do think I can say the following with a certain amount of confidence. At the core of our being as a collective, we have, from day one, been trying to wrestle with a myriad of things that were handed to us by our respective upbringings, ones that were steeped in very Christian traditions and ones that, depending on which member of the band we're talking about, we have either rejected completely and/or have wrestled with to the point that who we are now is not at all who we were years ago. Deconstruction, tearing down ideas, laying waste to the foundations, clearing the ground, and then attempting to rebuild bit by bit, reconfiguring how we thought about life, questions of doubt and faith, what it means to be human and humane . . . these were all ideas that we discussed from the beginning of the band and they run through each of our releases, albeit presented in different ways, depending on which facet we're focusing on.

The very name of the band, QOHELETH, is drawn directly from the book of Ecclesiastes, as the meanings of that word (collector, assembler, teacher) jumped out at me as we were discussing the animating themes behind our collective creative headspace. We are living in and through a period of confusion, contradiction, and upheaval. What is Ecclesiastes if not a reflection of those same themes? All is *hevel*, a vapor, meaningless, abstraction, all roads lead to the same place: death . . . and what is left of those who pass away? "The people of long ago are not remembered, no will there be any remembrance of people yet to come by those who come after them" (Eccl 1:11, NRSV). We pride ourselves on progress and superiority over nature, yet,

> For the fate of humans and the fate of animals is the same; as one dies, so dies the other. They all have the same breath, and humans have no advantage over the animals; for all is vanity. All go to one place; all are from the dust, and all turn to dust again. Who knows whether the human spirit goes upward and the spirit of animals goes downward to the earth? (Eccl 3:19–21, NRSV)

Of all the books in Scripture, I think that Ecclesiastes is the one that most steadfastly resists an easy read, or interpretations that make it a proof text for why life can be decoded in some easy manner, figured out and packaged in a digestible form. To be clear, I think the entirety of the Bible is actually like this, but certain passages within it, coupled with theological traditions that have flattened the texts, have led to portions of it being commodified to the point of near uselessness. Ecclesiastes, in the ways in which it is both plainly and poetically written, somehow seems to dodge that in a manner that I find incredibly life-giving. There are no easy answers here. It is full of contradiction, resignation, joy, hope, and yet a matter-of-factness about the human state of being that feels like getting dropped into the deep, rather than the safety of the shallows.

QOHELETH, *Black Kite Broadcasts* (2018)

Early on in our band's writing, Mike coined a phrase that's become a sort of rallying cry for us: "Written by accident, played by instinct." Strictly speaking, we are not an improvisational band. There is structure and intent woven into what we write, but usually, as we begin writing new songs and some of our longer form instrumental pieces, we approach our instruments with an openness to the sounds that come out of our amps. Rather than coming with a specific riff or musical movement in mind, I tend to mess around with amp and instrument settings and effects pedals until I land on a tone that captures my ear in the moment, and then begin stumbling across notes until a form starts taking place. Perhaps a simple pattern here, a sustained crash of noise there. It's an instinctual process and it's one that I think helps usher in a flexibility and willingness to dive into the inherent contradictions of mixing noise and music in some sort of weird beast of creativity.

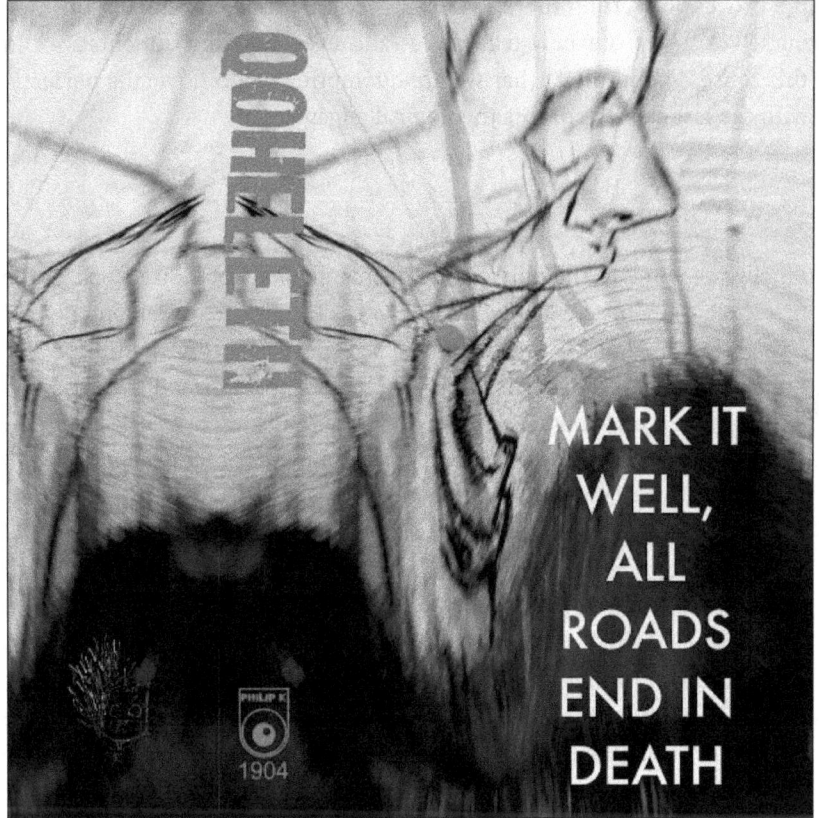

QOHELETH, *Mark It Well, All Roads End in Death* **(2019)**

Those contradictions are also reflected in the abstract visuals that Caiden paints for each of our releases. They are vibrant, alive, and yet largely resist formation into identifiable objects or scenes (minus a couple of key instances like *Black Kite Broadcasts* and *Mark It Well, All Roads End in Death*). This also allows the listener to view the art within their own framework, bringing their biases and perspectives with them, and figuring out how to converse on their own terms with the art that they are being presented with. The layers only increase when playing the music alongside the paintings, extending the overall experience into another dimension for grappling with the uncertainty that is our shared human existence. I wouldn't dare suggest that we've arrived as a band in terms of consistently nailing down exactly what we hope to express with each new song, or album, or EP. But I do believe we're getting more fluent in the process of getting there, while at the same time continually pushing ourselves to try out new techniques and even new instrumentation. In this sense, I think that what we are attempting to do dovetails perfectly with the last element of this theological engagement.

New Tongues

Finally, we come to the outworking of this theology of Noise/Rock. If the first three elements are largely internal areas for growth, development, and change, this final one is absolutely crucial for external communication and hope. If our ears, hearts, and minds are being transformed by noise and empathy, then our language itself will begin to change. We will have new opportunities to forge new language that can better describe, engage with, and talk about what we are experiencing as a species. If new wine can't possibly stay contained within old wineskins, how can we possibly expect old tongues to capture the new New of what we are beholding? The parable of old wineskins and new wine shows up in Matthew, Mark, and Luke, and while the context is specifically about wedding traditions and questions about fasting, I think the concept itself is perfect for what Noise/Rock suggests for forming new tongues. This is, in part, a key aspect of what we're aiming for with QOHELETH: new language that helps us better articulate the world(s) we're encountering. It's a ground clearing, another term (along with contradiction and ambiguity) that I keep returning to, over and over again. So much of this is a both/and, rather than an either/or. Our past frameworks have to evolve and change, or the old wineskins might burst, bringing about a new flood of nothingness that will overtake us.

Or perhaps it's already overtaken us and what we're experiencing right now is a combination of drowning and learning how to breathe underwater? Even in the depths, the *Sonus Dei* can find us and bring hope, if we can hear it and speak it. To that end, I want to close this out by focusing on a short film featuring Christine Sun Kim, a deaf sound/performance artist from the US. It was created by photographer and filmmaker Todd Selby and featured on the arts and storytelling website, *Nowness*.[21] As Selby followed Sun Kim throughout her day and in the process of creating a sound experience in a gallery exhibit, she revealed something truly profound, insights perhaps only visible to someone who has to feel sound, rather than hear it:

---

21. Selby, "Christine Sun Kim."

A THEOLOGY OF NOISE/ROCK

> While growing up, I constantly questioned the ownership of sound. People who have access to sound naturally own it and have a say in it. There were all these conventions for what was proper sound. They would tell me: be quiet. Don't burp, don't drag your feet, make loud noises. I learned to be respectful of their sound. I saw sound as their possession. Now I'm reclaiming sound as my property.[22]

Sun Kim goes on to explain that she didn't feel fully able to grasp any one language because her parents were trying to learn both English and Sign Language, and thus she was constantly left to make sense of fragments from both: "I didn't fully internalize or master any language because I didn't have full access to one."[23] Ultimately, this struggle led her to sound and noise:

> My work deals with the physicality of sound, a loose translation of sound to another form . . . and it incorporates performance. I want to explore sound without a mediated interpretation of what sound is. I want to find its meaning through my experience . . . I love creating feedback. It's one of my favorite sounds. Feedback can often be fierce and rough, which sends vibrations through my body. It becomes physical. It moves my body.[24]

Once again, that theme of embodiment through noise returns and we see how deeply important it is to be fully present in our bodies, and how tuning into the noises and sounds around us invite us back into that space.

Sun Kim closes her reflection on sound with this: "Let's listen with our eyes and not just our ears. That would be the ideal. Let's look at the bigger picture."[25] Listening more attentively is not just the purview of the ears, but the eyes as well. Sound and noise being made more physical helps bridge the gaps between those two senses and brings us closer to the realities that we each inhabit. This is where a theology of Noise/Rock can lead us: noise as glossolalia, with different types of textures as tongues. As someone who is fluent (albeit rusty) in a second language, I know from firsthand experience how difficult learning that new language can be. It's overwhelming, it's tiring, it's frustrating, it's maddening, it's humbling, and on and on and on.

And yet . . .

Whole new worlds, as clichéd as that sounds, open up with each new foothold in that foreign tongue. We gain the ability not only to speak in a

---

22. Selby, "Christine Sun Kim."
23. Selby, "Christine Sun Kim."
24. Selby, "Christine Sun Kim."
25. Selby, "Christine Sun Kim."

new language, but to think and even dream in it. On some level, the very appreciation of new cultures can only be achieved by knowing the language backwards and forwards, as it is within the language itself that humor and slang is housed, liberation and transgression in sonic form. By pushing us past our frameworks of how structural music is supposed to operate, noise can open up new pathways, inviting both a deepening appreciation for form, but also the joys and freedom of breaking out of it. It's a calling to more fully see and be seen. Noise/Rock is that invitation.

Epilogue

PLAYLIST:

Where do you want to go from here?

Scan for . . . ??

FROM CHAOS TO AMBIGUITY

In the end, this whole process has been in the pursuit of one thing: making room for all the things that we constantly tell ourselves and others that we need to get rid of.

Noise.

Discordance.

Incongruity.

Ambiguity.

Contradiction.

If we get rid of these things, we risk getting rid of key aspects of what makes us human. And paradoxically, they push us farther away from the Divine that embraced our finiteness and became one of us.

As I bring this to a close, the one thought that keeps resounding in my brain is: THERE IS SO MUCH WORK YET TO BE DONE. I've touched on it here and there throughout the journey thus far, but truly, there is so much left to be explored and discussed:

- Other noise rock scenes beyond the borders of the US.
- A study of key labels that helped bring these groups to the listeners.
- An in-depth look at the non-white, non-male fronted bands in the genre.
- Questions of how the early church perceived noise.
- A survey of key bands within particular regions of the US.
- The relationship between noise and *hevel*, the primary image/metaphor of Ecclesiastes.

My hope is that I've provided some semblance of a foothold for future writers and researchers to build upon. I offer it as a humble gift because I believe whole-heartedly in what I have wrestled with for the past few thousand words. Music is life, noise is joy, chaos is energy, and humanity is utterly beautiful and ugly and broken and good.

I can't for one second pretend to know for certain what exists beyond the horizon of our shared finiteness (I guess it's that pesky, damn question of faith all over and over again), yet when I am lost in what others have created and gifted to us, I can hear past and through it all. There is something, someone waiting for us on the other side. But none of us will make it there alone.

And the beauty of the noise is that none of us have to. It is us and God reflecting back onto ourselves and Godself reflected back on creation. How desperately we need to hear and be reminded. Feedback come and rain down on us.

Appendix
Music Timelines

The timelines presented here are meant to be a supplement to chapter 2 on the history of Punk and No Wave, leading into the formation of what became Noise Rock. While this is far from complete and/or exhaustive, especially as it concerns the existence of bands in these genres outside of the United States, this should be more than enough to help situate us in the ebb and flow of the development of these genres. The bands presented here each made an important contribution to their scenes and communities, while also adding their voices to these genres, expanding and developing the boundaries of said genres. The texts that cover specific bands, locales, and timeframes are mentioned in parenthetical notation (**bolded** and *italicized*) next to the years that they encapsulate. They are also cited fully in the Bibliography that follows.

    1965-1968 (NYC Punk = ***Please Kill Me***)

        Velvet Underground—*The Velvet Underground and Nico* (1966)

            —*White Light/White Heat* (1968)

    1967-1971 (NYC Punk, No Wave)

        Suicide (1970/71-2016)

    1971-1974 (NYC Punk, LA Punk = ***We Got The Neutron Bomb***)

        Death (1971-1977, 2009-present)—Detroit

        Devo (1973-1991, 1996-present)

APPENDIX: MUSIC TIMELINES

Patti Smith (1974–present)—NYC

1974–1975 (NYC Punk, *Revenge of the She-Punks*)

Lou Reed—*Metal Machine Music* (1975)

Blondie (1974–1982, 1997–present)—NYC

1976–1977 (NYC Punk, No Wave, LA Punk, *Our Band Could Be Your Life*, ROTSP)

The Gynecologists (1976–1978)

Teenage Jesus and the Jerks (1976–1979)

The Runaways (1975–1979)

The Screamers (1975–1981)

X-Ray Spex (1976–1979, 1991, 1995–1996, 2008)—London

The Germs (1976–1980, 2005–2009, 2013)

Black Flag (1976–1986, 2003, 2013–2014, 2019–present)

Mars (1977–1978)

Red Transistor (1977–1978)

Theoretical Girls (1977–1981)

DNA (1977–1982)

Crass (1977–1984)—Epping, Essex

The Raincoats (1977–1984, 1993–present)—London

Contortions (1977–2016)

X (1977–present)

Fear (1977–present)

Bad Brains (1977–1995, 1998–present)—DC

1978–1980 (NYC Punk, No Wave, LA Punk, OBCBYL)

No New York (1978)

Ut (1978–1990)

Beirut Slump (1978–1979)

The Go-Go's (1978–1985, 1990, 1994, 1999–present)

8 Eyed Spy (1979–1980)

APPENDIX: MUSIC TIMELINES

Bush Tetras (1979-1983)

Hüsker Dü (1979-1988)—St. Paul

The Replacements (1979-1991, 2006, 2012-2015)—Minneapolis

Dark Day (1979-2005)

Mission of Burma (1979-1983, 2002-2016)—Boston

Social Distortion (1979-Present)

Agent Orange (1979-present)

Flipper (1979-1987, 1990-1993, 2005-present)

1980-1992 (NYC Punk, No Wave, LA Punk, OBCBYL)

Adolescents (1980-1981, 1986-1989, 2001-present)

Minor Threat (1980-1983)—DC

The Minutemen (1980-1985)

Sonic Youth (1981-2011)

Butthole Surfers (1981-present)—San Antonio

Beat Happening (1982-present)—Olympia

Scratch Acid (1982-1987, 2006, 2011)—Austin

Swans (1982-1997, 2010-2017, 2019-present)

Live Skull (1982-1990, 2016-present)

Killdozer (1983-1996)—Madison

Dinosaur Jr. (1984-1997, 2005-present)—Amherst

1986 (OBCBYL)

Fugazi (1986-2003)—DC

God Bullies (1986-1995)—Kalamazoo

1987 (Book)

The Jesus Lizard (1987-1999, 2008-2010, 2017-present)
—Austin & Chicago

Barkmarket (1987-1997)—NYC

Cows (1987-1998)—Minneapolis

1988 (OBCBYL)

Slug (1988–1996)—LA

Unsane (1988–2000, 2003–2019)—NYC

Mudhoney (1988–present)—Seattle

1989 (Thin Black Book)

Oxbow (1989–present)—San Francisco

1989–1992 (Girls To The Front)

Bikini Kill (1990–1997, 2017, 2019–present)—Olympia

Drive Like Jehu (1990–1995, 2014–2016)—San Diego

Bratmobile (1991–1994, 1998–2003)—Olympia

Heavens to Betsy (1991–1994)—Olympia

Huggy Bear (1991–1994)—London/Brighton

Cherubs (1991–1994, 2014–present)—Austin

1999

Hot Snakes (1999–2005, 2011–present)—San Diego

2000

Part Chimp (2000–2011, 2016–present)—London

2007

Le Butcherettes (2007–present)—Guadalajara

Bibliography

Azerrad, Michael. *Our Band Could Be Your Life: Scenes from the American Indie Underground 1981-1991*. New York: Back Bay, 2001.
Begbie, Jeremy. *Voicing Creation's Praise: Towards a Theology of the Arts*. London: Bloomsbury T&T Clark, 2000.
Buechner, Frederick. *The Alphabet of Grace*. New York: HarperCollins, 1970.
Callaway, Kutter, and Dean Batali. *Watching TV Religiously: Television and Theology in Dialogue*. Grand Rapids: Baker Academics, 2016.
Callaway, Kutter, and Barry Taylor. *The Aesthetics of Atheism*. Minneapolis: Fortress, 2019.
Caputo, John D. *The Folly of God: A Theology of the Unconditional*. Salem, OR: Polebridge, 2016.
Christgau, Robert. "Township Jive Conquers the World." *Village Voice*, March 3, 1987. Online. https://www.robertchristgau.com/xg/pnj/pj86.php.
Ciocca, Morgan. "Basquiat Decorates Time and Space in New Showcase from The Broad." *Vocalo*, January 21, 2021. Online. https://vocalo.org/basquiat-thebroad.
Cone, James H. *A Black Theology of Liberation*. Maryknoll, NY: Orbis, 2010.
———. *The Spirituals and the Blues: An Interpretation*. Maryknoll, NY: Orbis, 1992.
Dante Alighieri. *The Divine Comedy*. Translated by Allen Mandelbaum. New York: Alfred A. Knopf, 1995.
Dault, David "To The Void: Karl Barth, Yves Klein, and Lou Reed's *Metal Machine Music*." In *Secular Music & Sacred Theology*, edited by Tom Beaudoin, 3-15. Collegeville, MN: Liturgical, 2013.
Davies, Oliver. "Dante's *Commedia* and the Body of Christ." In *Dante's "Commedia": Theology as Poetry*, edited by Vittorio Montemaggi and Matthew Treherne, 161-79. Notre Dame: University of Notre Dame, 2010.
Dyrness, William A. *Poetic Theology: God and the Poetics of Everyday Life*. Grand Rapids: Eerdmans, 2011.
Farrell, Michael P. *Collaborative Circles: Friendship Dynamics & Creative Work*. Chicago: University of Chicago Press, 2001.
Gaines, Donna. *Teenage Wasteland: Suburbia's Dead End Kids*. Chicago: University of Chicago Press, 1998.

Goldman, Vivien. *Revenge of the She-Punks: A Feminist Music History from Poly Styrene to Pussy Riot*. Austin: University of Texas Press, 2019.

Hainge, Greg. *Noise Matters: Towards an Ontology of Noise*. New York: Bloomsbury Academic, 2013.

Hard, Mike. "God Bullies, Thrall, They Never Sleep." *Conan Neutron's Protonic Reversal*, February 21, 2021. Episode 231. Online. https://www.protonicreversal.com/2021/02/21/ep231-mike-hard-god-bullies-thrall-they-never-sleep-2.

Hart, Trevor "Through the Arts: Hearing, Seeing and Touching the Truth." In *Beholding the Glory: Incarnation through the Arts*, edited by Jeremy Begbie, 1–26. Grand Rapids: Baker, 2001.

Hegarty, Paul. *Noise/Music: A History*. New York: Bloomsbury Academic, 2007.

Host, Vivian. "Le Butcherettes' Teri Gender Bender on Discovering Punk and Feminism." *New Noise Magazine*, August 12, 2016. Online. https://daily.redbullmusicacademy.com/2016/08/teri-gender-bender-interview.

Iafrate, Michael J. "More Than Music: Notes on 'Staying Punk' in the Church and in Theology." In *Secular Music & Sacred Theology*, edited by Tom Beaudoin, 35–58. Collegeville, MN: Liturgical, 2013.

Johnston, Robert K. *God's Wider Presence: Reconsidering General Revelation*. Ada, MI: Baker Academic, 2014.

Keuss, Jeffrey F. "Tom Waits, Nick Cave, and Martin Heidegger: On Singing of the God Who Will Not Be Named." In *Secular Music & Sacred Theology*, edited by Tom Beaudoin, 149–66. Collegeville, MN: Liturgical, 2013.

Kroneiss, Rich. "Circling the Pile: An Interview with Tom Hazelmyer." *Terminal Boredom*, n.d. Online. http://www.terminal-boredom.com/hazexxl.html.

Marsh, Clive, and Vaughn S. Roberts. *Personal Jesus: How Popular Music Shapes Our Souls*. Ada, MI: Baker Academic, 2012.

Marcus, Sara. *Girls to the Front: The True Story of the Riot Grrrl Revolution*. New York: Harper Perennial, 2010.

Masters, Marc. *No Wave*. London: Black Dog, 2007.

McNeil, Legs, and Gillian McCain. *Please Kill Me: The Uncensored Oral History of Punk*. 20th anniversary ed. New York: Grove, 2016.

Novak, Michael. *The Experience of Nothingness*. New York: Routledge, 2017.

O'Connor, Flannery. *The Complete Stories*. New York: Farrar, Straus and Giroux, 1971.

Partridge, Christopher. *The Lyre of Orpheus: Popular Music, The Sacred, & The Profane*. Oxford: Oxford University Press, 2014.

Prindle, Mark. "David B. Livingstone." *Mark's Record Reviews*, 2004. Online. http://www.markprindle.com/livingstone-i.htm.

Quash, Ben. *Found Theology: History, Imagination, and the Holy Spirit*. Edinburgh: T&T Clark, 2014.

Rieff, Philip. *My Life Among the Deathworks: Illustrations of the Aesthetics of Authority*. Sacred Order/Social Order 1. Charlottesville: University of Virginia Press, 2006.

Robinson, Eugene S. "The Complicated Case For And Against O. J. Simpson." *OZY*, June 9, 2019. Online. https://www.ozy.com/true-story/the-complicated-case-for-and-against-oj-simpson/94303.

———. "Grisly John Wayne Gacy, the Painting, Murdering Clown." *OZY*, May 5, 2019. Online. https://www.ozy.com/flashback/grisly-john-wayne-gacy-the-painting-murdering-clown/94082.

———. "Interview." *Burning Ambulance*, January 9, 2013. Online. https://burningambulance.com/2013/01/09/interview-eugene-robinson.

———. *Thin Black Book*. Los Angeles: Hydra Head Records, 2017.

———. "When Albanian Singers Crushed the World." *OZY*, June 6, 2019. Online. https://www.ozy.com/fast-forward/when-albanian-singers-crushed-the-world/94412.

———. "When Sex Workers Were Hookers." *OZY*, April 25, 2019. Online. https://www.ozy.com/flashback/when-sex-workers-were-hookers/93634.

———. "When What Happened to Rodney King Changed Everything." *OZY*, April 28, 2019. Online. https://www.ozy.com/true-story/when-what-happened-to-rodney-king-changed-everything/93964.

Roglieri, Maria Ann. "Twentieth-Century Musical Interpretations of the 'Anti-Music' of Dante's *Inferno*." *Italica* 79.2 (2002) 149–67.

Savage, Sara B. "Through Dance: Fully Human, Fully Alive." In *Beholding the Glory: Incarnation through the Arts*, edited by Jeremy Begbie, 64–82. Grand Rapids: Baker, 2000.

Selby, Todd. "Christine Sun Kim." *Nowness*, November 8, 2011. Online. https://www.nowness.com/story/todd-selby-x-christine-sun-kim.

Siedell, Daniel A. *Who's Afraid of Modern Arts? Essays on Modern Art and Theology in Conversation*. Eugene, OR: Cascade, 2015.

Silva, John. "Le Butcherettes On Legends, Symbolism & New Album *bi/MENTAL*." *New Noise Magazine*, February 4, 2019. Online. https://newnoisemagazine.com/le-butcherettes-on-legends-symbolism-new-album-bi-mental.

Sisario, Ben. "The Art of Noise." *Spin Magazine*, December 2, 2004. Online. https://www.spin.com/2004/12/art-noise.

Spitz, Marc, and Brendan Mullen. *We Got the Neutron Bomb: The Untold Story of LA Punk*. NYC: Three Rivers, 2001.

Sorett, Josef. *Spirit in the Dark: A Religious History of Racial Aesthetics*. Oxford: Oxford University Press, 2016.

Stephenson, Ken. *What to Listen for in Rock: A Stylistic Analysis*. New Haven, CT: Yale University Press, 2002.

Tanner, Aaron. *Butthole Surfers: What Does Regret Mean?* Evansville, IN: Melodic Virtue, 2019.

Tanner, Kathryn. *Theories of Culture: A New Agenda for Theology*. Minneapolis: Fortress, 1997.

Terich, Jeff. "Hold on to Your Genre: Noise Rock." *Treblezine*, February 25, 2013. Online. https://www.treblezine.com/hold-on-to-your-genre-noise-rock.

Thacker, Eugene. *In the Dust of This Planet*. Horror of Philosophy 1. London: Zero, 2010.

The Jesus Lizard. *The Jesus Lizard Book*. Brooklyn: Akashic, 2013.

Thomas, Kenneth. "Blood, Sweat, and Vinyl: DIY in the 21st Century (Trailer)." April 23, 2013. Online. https://www.youtube.com/watch?v=mnTdKkeqzMg.

Vee, Tesco, and Dave Stimson. *Touch and Go: The Complete Hardcore Punk Zine '79–'83*. Edited by Steve Miller. Brooklyn: Bazillion Points, 2010.

Discography

Barkmarket. "Dumbjaw." Track 4 on *Gimmick*. American Recordings 9 45343-2, 1993, compact disc.

Barkmarket. "Visible Cow." Track 1 on *L. Ron*. American Recordings 9 43071-2, 1996, compact disc.

Big Black. "Kerosene." Track 4 on *Atomizer*. Homestead Records HMS043, 1986, vinyl record.

Big Business. "Heal the Weak." Track 2 on *The Beast You Are*. Joyful Noise Recordings JNR295, Gold Metal Records JNR295, 2019, compact disc.

The Birthday Party. "Release the Bats." Track 13 on *Junkyard*. 2.13.61 Records thi 21317.2, 1997, compact disc.

Black Flag. "Six Pack." Track 1 on *Six Pack*. SST Records SST 005, 1981, vinyl record.

Brandy. "Clown Pain." Track 1 on *Clown Pain*. Total Punk TPR 65, 2019, vinyl record.

Buñuel. "This Is Love." Track 2 on *A Resting Place for Strangers*. La Tempesta International LTI 028/16, 2016, compact disc.

Buñuel. "Jesus with a Cock." Track 4 on *A Resting Place for Strangers*. La Tempesta International LTI 028/16, 2016, compact disc.

Le Butcherettes. "Tainted In Sin." Track 10 on *Sin Sin Sin*. Rodriguez Lopez Productions RLP012, 2011, compact disc.

Le Butcherettes. "Demon Stuck In Your Eye." Track 2 on *Cry Is for the Flies*. Ipecac Recordings IPC161, 2014, compact disc.

Le Butcherettes. "give/UP." Track 2 on *bi/MENTAL*. Rise Records RISE 415-2, 2019, compact disc.

Butthole Surfers. "Moving to Florida." Track 1 on *Cream Corn from the Socket of Davis*. Touch and Go T&G 14, 1985, vinyl record.

Butthole Surfers. "Who Was in My Room Last Night?" Track 1 on *Independent Worm Saloon*. Capitol Records CDP 0777 7 98798 2 3, 1993, compact disc.

Butthole Surfers. "Pepper." Track 3 on *Electriclarryland*. Capitol Records CDP 7243 8 29842 2 1, 1996, compact disc.

Celan. "All This And Everything." Track 3 on *Halo*. Exile On Mainstream Records EOM041, 2009, compact disc.

DISCOGRAPHY

The Chariot. "Cheek." Track 10 on *One Wing*. Entertainment One EOM-CD-2439, 2012, compact disc.

Cherubs. "Monkey Chow Mein." Track 3 on *2 Ynfynyty*. Brutal Panda Records BPR27, 2015, cassette tape.

Cows. "Tourist." Track 9 on *Taint Pluribus Taint Unum*. Treehouse Records TR 007, 1987, vinyl record.

Cows. "Hitting the Wall." Track 1 on *Peacetika*. Amphetamine Reptile Records AmRep 001, 1991, cassette tape.

Crystal Fairy. "Drugs On The Bus." Track 2 on *Crystal Fairy*. Ipecac Recordings IPC180, 2017, compact disc.

Culturcide. "The Heart of R 'n' R (Is the Profit)." Track 7 on *Tacky Souvenirs Of Pre-Revolutionary America*. Not On Label (Culturcide Self-released), 1986, vinyl record.

Death. "Politicians In My Eyes." Track 7 on *. . . For the Whole World to See*. Drag City DC387CD, 2009, compact disc.

The Go-Go's. "We Got The Beat." Track 6 on *Beauty and the Beat*. IRS Records SP 70021, 1981, vinyl record.

God Bullies. "Act of Desire." Track 1 on *Mama Womb Womb*. Amphetamine Reptile Records ARR 89157-1, 1989, vinyl record.

God Bullies. "Let's Go To Hell." Track 1 on *Dog Show*. Amphetamine Reptile Records ARR 89181-2, 1990, compact disc.

God Bullies. "Monster Jesus." Track 2 on *Dog Show*. Amphetamine Reptile Records ARR 89181-2, 1990, compact disc.

God Bullies. "Neighborhood Kid." Track 1 on *Kill the King*. Alternative Tentacles VIRUS 152CD, 1994, compact disc.

God Bullies. "King of Sling." Track 2 on *Kill the King*. Alternative Tentacles VIRUS 152CD, 1994, compact disc.

God Bullies. "How Many Times." Track 3 on *Kill the King*. Alternative Tentacles VIRUS 152CD, 1994, compact disc.

God Bullies. "Detain My Brain." Track 4 on *Kill the King*. Alternative Tentacles VIRUS 152CD, 1994, compact disc.

God Bullies. "Artificial Insemination by Aliens." Track 10 on *Kill the King*. Alternative Tentacles VIRUS 152CD, 1994, compact disc.

God Bullies. "Hate." Track 11 on *Kill the King*. Alternative Tentacles VIRUS 152CD, 1994, compact disc.

The Jesus Lizard. "Happy Bunny Goes Fluff Fluff Along." Track 15 on *Head/Pure*. Touch and Go TG454CD, 2012, compact disc.

The Jesus Lizard. "Mouth Breather." Track 2 on *Goat*. Touch and Go TG468CD, 2009, compact disc.

The Jesus Lizard. "Nub." Track 3 on *Goat*. Touch and Go TG468CD, 2009, compact disc.

Mars. "Tunnel." Track 3 on *78*. Widowspeak Productions WSP 10, 1986, vinyl record.

MC5. "Ramblin' Rose." Track 1 on *Kick Out the Jams*. Elektra EKS-74042, 1969, vinyl record.

Melvins. "The Talking Horse." Track 1 on *(A) Senile Animal*. Ipecac Recordings IPC82, 2006, compact disc.

Melvins feat. Teri Gender Bender. "Rebel Girl." Track 1 on *Rebel Girl*. Joyful Noise Recordings JNR 208-1, 2015, lathe cut record.

Minutemen. "The Glory of Man." Track 21 on *Double Nickels on the Dime*. SST Records SST CD 028, 1987, compact disc.

DISCOGRAPHY

Oxbow. "Shine [Glimmer]." Track 9 on *An Evil Heat*. Neurot Recordings NR017, 2002, compact disc.
Oxbow. "Frank's Frolic." Track 8 on *The Narcotic Story*. Hydra Head Records HH666-112, 2007, compact disc.
Oxbow. "A Cold and Well-Lit Place." Track 1 on *Thin Black Duke*. Hydra Head Records HHR228 CD, 2017, compact disc.
Oxbow. "A Gentleman's Gentleman." Track 3 on *Thin Black Duke*. Hydra Head Records HHR228 CD, 2017, compact disc.
Oxbow. "Letter of Note." Track 4 on *Thin Black Duke*. Hydra Head Records HHR228 CD, 2017, compact disc.
Oxbow. "The Upper." Track 6 on *Thin Black Duke*. Hydra Head Records HHR228 CD, 2017, compact disc.
Oxbow. "Other People." Track 7 on *Thin Black Duke*. Hydra Head Records HHR228 CD, 2017, compact disc.
Part Chimp. "30,000,000,000,000,000 People." Track 10 on *I Am Come*. Monitor Records MON027, 2005, compact disc.
QOHELETH. "Brood of Vipers." Track 2 on *God Is the Warmest Place to Hide*. Not On Label (Qoheleth Self-released), 2017, compact disc.
QOHELETH. "Uterine." Track 3 on *Black Kite Broadcasts*. Bad Cake Records 009, 2018, cassette tape.
QOHELETH. "These Exquisitely Dressed Trees." Track 1 on *Mark It Well, All Roads End in Death*. Philip K. Discs 1904, 2019, cassette tape.
Ramones. "Judy Is a Punk." Track 3 on *Ramones*. Sire SASD-7520, 1976, vinyl record.
Sonic Youth. "I Dreamed I Dream." Track 2 on *Sonic Youth*. Neutral Records N-ONE, 1982, vinyl record.
Shakuhachi Surprise. "Swavay." Track 1 on *Space Streakings Sighted over Mount Shasta*. Skin Graft Records GR 35CD, 1996, compact disc.
Shellac. "Didn't We Deserve a Look at You the Way You Really Are." Track 1 on *Terraform*. Touch and Go TG 200 CD, 1998, compact disc.
STNNNG. "Grand Island, Neb." Track 1 on *Fake Fake*. Modern Radio Record Label MRRL-035, 2006, compact disc.
The Stooges. "I Wanna Be Your Dog." Track 2 on *The Stooges*. Elektra EKS-74051, 1969, vinyl record.
Swans. "Stay Here." Track 1 on *Filth*. Neutral Records N11, 1983, vinyl record.
Teenage Jesus and the Jerks. "Orphans." Track 1 on *Orphans*. Migraine CC-333, 1978, vinyl record.
Thrice. "Death From Above." Track 9 on *To Be Everywhere Is to Be Nowhere*. Vagrant Records VR4391, 2016, compact disc.
Unsane. "Scrape." Track 1 on *Scattered, Smothered & Covered*. Amphetamine Reptile Records AmRep 039-2, 1995, compact disc.

www.ingramcontent.com/pod-product-compliance
Lightning Source LLC
Chambersburg PA
CBHW050817160426
43192CB00010B/1791